Introduction

This book introduces some new cutters, a ve
superb frilling tools and makes use of some
tools in the ORCHARD PRODUCTS range, a
in this series - Books 1 to 6.

Book 5 'Great Ideas for Cake Decorators' IS
comprehensive index to all the the Books 1 to 5.

References: Throughout the book reference is made to 'glue', which is intended to mean Triple strength Rose Water or Gum Arabic glue. 'Paste' Glue is also included where appropriate, since it can make undetectable joins. Egg white may be used if required. Similarly 'paste' means flowerpaste, unless otherwise specified.

The Tools. General Notes:

Non-stick.   One of their most useful aspects is their non-stick property, which is inherent in the design and material used. It is not a surface finish and, therefore, cannot wear off. It also means they cut cleanly, without fuzzy edges.

Materials   All the tools can be used with any soft material such as flowerpaste, sugarpaste, marzipan, modelling chocolate, plasticine, modelling clay etc.

Temperature.   They will withstand boiling water or the dishwasher without deforming.

Handles.   All the cutters have comfortably sized handles which allow you to exert firm pressure over the whole of the cutting edges.

Stability.   They will not rust, corrode, deform or wear out with normal useage.

Marking.   All the tools are permanently marked to aid easy identification.

Metal.   They should not be brought into contact with sharp metal objects which may damage the cutting edges or surfaces, i.e. keep them separated from metal cutters.

Boards.   Our original non-stick boards (white or green) with their rubber feet and non-stick rolling pins (5" to 23") really do make handling sticky materials more of a pleasure and enable you to roll out your pastes much thinner than you thought possible.

Hygiene.   The materials meet the appropriate EEC regulations for food hygiene.

Endorsement.   All the items are personally endorsed and used by PAT ASHBY, our Technical Director, who is one of the leading teachers of sugarcraft in the UK and is an International judge and demonstrator.

THE NEW CUTTERS *(See Illustration 1).*
(Full size shapes are shown in Illustration 2).
1. The Six-petal cutters (N1,N2,N3,N4,N5,N6,N7,N8). This attractive range of cutters enables a variety of flowers to be made easily including Narcissus, lily, clematis etc. A selection of delightful flowers made with these cutters is shown in the book.
2. Lady's Face (HD2). This face complements our existing child's face (HD1), and it is put to good use in this book on the wedding cake and on the lady's face plaques. You will probably have even better ideas.

THE NEW TOOLS (See Illustration 3).
The Folding Flowerstand (S1). The prototype of this design was made several years ago by Ken and Betty Debnam of Tasmania, and Pat Ashby has also been using it for eighteen months. It has therefore been well proven in practice. It has 98 tapered holes of different sizes, spaced to avoid the larger flowers from touching each other and thus getting damaged. It has a rail to hang your fuchsia's and the like from. This version has folding legs, which makes it one of the few flowerstands you can get into your workbox.
Mexican Hat Adaptor (M1). This adaptor can be used on its own or clicked onto the end of the Flower Stand (See Illustration 3). Push a small ball of paste over a suitably sized hole with your thumb and remove the resulting Mexican Hat!
Roll out the brim as usual.
For cutters without a suitable hole in the back, petals can be cut out with the 'hat' still in the hole.
Frilling Tools (FT1,FT2,FT3,FT4). This set of 4 non-stick tools solves a perennial problem of finding suitably small but rigid enough tools to frill quickly and easily, with variations, to enhance all your frill work.

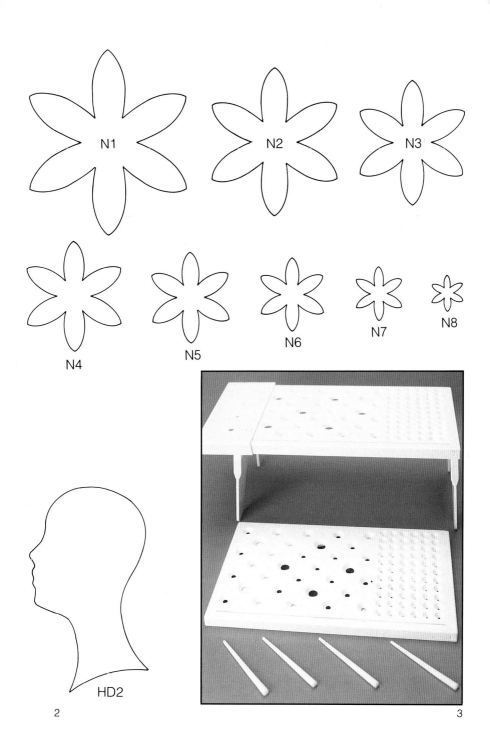

N1

N2

N3

N4

N5

N6

N7

N8

HD2

2

3

4

Tiger Lily - Harmony - *Lilum Tigrinum* (See Illustration 4).

1. Stamens (6 required). To colour the wire, put Orange colour onto a sponge, grip a piece of fine scientific covered wire in the sponge and pull through. Leave to dry. Cut to $3/4$ of the length of the petal (N1).

Mash some Brown paste with a little rose water or water to form a 'glue' paste. Dip the end of each wire into this glue and push into the side of a tiny sausage of Brown paste (about 4mm ($1/8$") long). Leave to dry.

2. Piston. Push a ball of Orange paste onto the glued end of a piece of the Orange scientific wire (as above). When dry this is taped into the centre of the stamens but protudes slightly above them. When taped up the brown part of the stamens all line up in the same way (see Diagram 6).

3. Petals. Make a 'Mexican Hat' of Orange flowerpaste by pushing a small ball of paste over a suitably sized hole in the Mexican Hat Adaptor (M1) with your thumb and remove. Roll out the brim, place the N1 cutter over the crown of the 'hat' and cut out 1– six petal flower.

5

6

4. Hold the crown of the hat between your thumb and forefinger, lay a petal over your finger and widen out the base of each alternate petal with the petal veining tool (OP2) by putting the point of the tool at the base, pressing firmly and rolling the tool from side to side. Vein the remainder of the petal by rolling the tool over it gently.

Vein the remaining petals in the same way.

The widened petals are on the inside when assembled.

5. Place the 'Hat' crown uppermost on the Orchard Pad (PD1) and make two grooves down the centre of each petal with the single end of the veining tool. One goes all the way down the centre to the point and the other goes at the side (See Illustration 5). Soften the edges with the balling tool.

6. Holding the stem in your fingers, press the veining tool into the centre of the flower to make a recess for the stamens. Put a little glue onto the base of the stamens and thread through the centre of the flower. Squeeze at the base and roll between your finger and thumb. Pop into the flowerstand (S1) and prop the petals with 'cloud drift'* so that they bend right back. Leave to dry.

7. Leaves. Roll Light Green paste into a tapered sausage, flatten out, leaving one end a little thicker, and just mark the centre and either side with the single end of the veining tool(OP2).

Push a glued 33 gauge wire into the thicker end, curve and leave to dry.

8. Paint the spots and the grooves in the petals a darker Orange. Twirl briefly in the steam of a boiling kettle to give it the 'waxy' look.

9. Buds. Roll out a sausage in White paste, tapered at one end. Push a 26 gauge glued wire into the non-tapered end. Pinch several grooves round the bud with tweezers and cut through the very tip with a knife. Make a few more grooves with the single end of the petal veining tool.

When dry, dust with Pale Yellow and Green. The largest buds are slightly Pink.

* 'Cloud Drift' is teased out Acrylic fibre as used in stuffed toys or in your duvet!

7

8

Winter Jasmine *(See Illustration 7).*

1. Tape a small Green stamen onto the end of a 33 gauge wire.

2. Flowerpaste - colour Bitter Lemon with a touch of Egg Yellow. Make a Mexican Hat (as described on Page 2) and cut out 1-N5 six petal flower.

3. Hold the crown of the hat between your thumb and forefinger, lay a petal over your finger and widen out each petal with the petal veining tool (OP2) by putting the point of the tool at the base, pressing firmly and rolling the tool from side to side. Place on the Orchard Pad (PD1) and soften the edges with the balling tool.

4. Make a recess in the centre of the flower with a cocktail stick and press against each petal. Glue the base of the stamen and thread through the centre of the flower, then taper the stem by rolling between your finger and thumb. Place in the flowerstand (S1) and leave to dry. (See Illustration 8).

5. Calyx. Cut out 1-R15 Small calyx from Green paste. Place on the Orchard Pad (PD1) and soften the edges with the balling tool. Glue the base of the flower and thread the calyx onto the wire. Press gently into position at the base of the tapered end of the Mexican Hat.

6. Small Buds. Push a tapered Green sausage of paste onto the glued end of a 33 gauge wire. Cut out 1-R15 Small calyx, glue the bud, thread the calyx onto the wire and wrap round the bud. When dry, dust the tip with Red.

7. Large Buds. Push a cone of Yellow paste onto the glued end of a 33 gauge wire. Roll the centre between your fingers to form a tapered sausage. Leave to dry.

Calyx for bud. Proceed as for Step 5 above and wrap round.

9

10

Pear Blossom. *(See Illustration 9).*

1. Tape 16 White stamens onto the end of a 28 gauge wire with Green florists tape. Spread them out and colour the tips with Mulberry colour.

2. Roll out White paste and cut out 1-F7 five-petal flower. Transfer it to the Orchard Pad (PD1), vein each petal by rolling the petal veining tool (OP2) over it and ball each petal with the balling tool (OP1) to soften the edges.

3. Pop onto a soft sponge and cup by pressing in the centre with the balling tool.

4. Place it in the flower stand (S1) and press gently with the balling tool to cup and interleave the petals. Apply a little glue to the base of the stamens and thread the wire through the centre of the flower. Leave to dry. (See Illustration 10).

5. Calyx. Roll out Green paste and cut out 1- R15 (Small calyx). Pop it on the pad and ball each sepal from the outside to the centre to curl them. Apply glue to the base of the flower, thread the calyx onto the wire and press up round the base of the flower.

6. Take a tiny ball of Green paste and glue it underneath the calyx. Thin it down the wire by rolling between your finger and thumb.

7. Bud. Hook the end of a 28 gauge wire and glue a ball of White paste onto the hooked end. Leave to dry.

8. Roll out White paste and cut out 1-F9 Five-petal flower. Vein the petals with the veining tool (OP2), turn over onto the pad (PD1) and ball each petal on the outside edge. Transfer to soft sponge and cup in the centre.

9. Glue the ball and thread the flower onto the wire such that the veining is on the outside. Wrap the petals over the top of the ball. Leave to dry. Dust the tips Pale Pink.

10. Calyx. Roll out Green paste and cut out 1-R15 (Small calyx). Pop it on the pad and ball each sepal from the outside to the centre to curl them. Apply glue to the base of the bud, thread the calyx onto the wire and press up round the base of the bud.

11. Take a tiny ball of Green paste and glue it underneath the calyx. Thin it down the wire by rolling between your finger and thumb.

12. Pear Leaf. Roll out a fat tapered sausage of Green paste, flatten, leaving a thickened end. Roll out from the centre and mark veins with the veining tool (OP2).

13. Glue the end of a 33 gauge wire for a small leaf (28 gauge for a larger leaf) and push into the thickened end. Ball round the outside edge to thin it down. Twist to shape when dry, dust with a little Moss Green and a tiny amount of Brown petal dust.

11

Japonica (*See Illustration 11*).

1. Tape 18 Yellow stamens onto a 26 gauge wire with Green florists tape. Spread out from the centre.

2. Cut out 1-F8 five-petal flower from Coral Pink flowerpaste. (For smaller flowers use F9). Vein the petals with the petal veining tool (OP2). Move it onto the Orchard Pad (PD1) and ball round just inside the edge of each petal with the balling tool (OP1).

3. Move it onto soft sponge and press in the centre with the balling tool to cup it.

4. Put the flower into the flowerstand (S1) and gently press in the centre with the balling tool. Apply rose water to the base of the stamens and thread through the centre of the flower. Leave to dry. (See Illustration 12).

12

5. Base of the flower. Roll out Pale Green flowerpaste into a sausage shape, tapered at the end. Mark all the way round in the centre with a knife. Apply rose water to the base of the flower and thread the wire through the centre of the sausage and press the end gently onto the base of the flower, tapering off the lower end by rolling between your fingers.

6. Leaves. Roll out a sausage shape from Green paste, tapered at both ends. Flatten and roll out from the centre to each side leaving a thickened end at the base. Soften the edge of the leaf with the balling tool.

7. Mark the main vein with the single end of the veining tool (OP2) and then either use a leaf mould (see Book 2 Page 28), stroke in the secondary veins with the veining tool, or press onto the underside of a real leaf.

8. Moisten the end of a 33 gauge wire with rose water and, holding the base of the leaf between your finger and thumb, push the wire into the thickened part. Shape and leave to dry. When dry, dust with a darker shade of Green.

13

Marigold (*See Illustration 13*).

1. Hook the end of a 28 gauge wire and then bend it back. Roll out Orange flowerpaste and cut out 2 - DY5 daisies. Vein each petal with the petal veining tool (OP2) - roll from the centre one way and then the other way to widen the petals.

2. Glue the centre with rose water and lay one cut-out on top of the other, alternating the petals. Pop onto the flower stand (S1) and press in the centre with the balling tool (OP1). Glue the hooked end of the wire and thread through the centre. Leave to dry.

3. Calyx. Roll out Green paste and cut out 1-N7 Six petal shape. Cut each petal in half along its length, apply glue to the base of the flower, thread the calyx onto the wire and press up round the flower.

4. When dry, glue a small ball of Brown paste into the centre of the flower. Make little indentations with a cocktail stick. Leave to dry.

'Marmalade' *(See Illustration 14).*

1. For the pointed version, proceed as Page 10 but with the N3 six petal cutter. Use 1-N8 six petal cutter for the calyx as for the Marigold. Put a ball of Black paste in the centre to finish.

Speciosum Rubrum Lily (*See Illustration 15*).

1. Stamens (6 required). Cut some White scientific wire pieces about $^3/_4$ length of the petals (N1). Mash some Orangey/Brown paste with a little rose water or water to form a 'glue' paste. Dip the end of each wire into this glue and push into the middle of a tiny sausage of Orangey/Brown paste (about 4mm: $^3/_4$" long). Colour just the top of the wires Pale Green. Leave to dry.

2. Piston. Glue the end of a 33 gauge wire with the paste glue and push into a small ball of Mauve flowerpaste. Pinch round three times with tweezers to form three distinct sections. When dry, tape into the centre of the stamens but make sure it protrudes above the stamens.

3. Petals. Make a 'Mexican Hat' of White flowerpaste by pushing a small ball of paste over a suitably sized hole in the Mexican Hat Adaptor (M1) with your thumb and remove. Roll out the brim, place the N1 cutter over the crown of the 'hat' and cut out 1– six petal flower.

4. Hold the crown of the hat between your thumb and forefinger, lay a petal over your finger and widen out the base of each alternate petal with the petal veining tool (OP2) by putting the point of the tool at the base, pressing firmly and rolling the tool from side to side. Vein the remainder of the petal by rolling the tool over it gently. (See Illustration 16).

Vein the remaining petals in the same way.

Press the veining tool into the middle of the flower to hollow out the centre.

16

5. Turn the 'hat' with the crown uppermost and pinch in from the crown to the end of each petal with tweezers to make a small ridge. Turn over and stoke a single vein down the centre of each petal with the veining tool.

Pop into the flowerstand (S1) and prop the petals with 'cloud drift'. The wider petals are inside when assembled.

6. Glue the base of the stamens and thread through the centre of the flower. Leave to dry.

7. When dry, paint and dust the various markings as can be seen from Illustration 15. The Green is applied first and then the Pink etc. Paint spots with a '000' paint brush.

8. Buds. The small bud is a tapered sausage of Pale Green paste pushed onto the glued end of a 26 gauge wire. Mark grooves on the outside with the single end of the veining tool.

The large bud is a tapered sausage of White paste pushed onto the glued end of a 26 gauge wire. Pinch from the bottom to the top with tweezers to make little ridges. When dry, dust a tiny amount of Green at the bottom, and Pink and Yellow around top and sides.

17

18

Clematis - 'Gypsy Queen' (*See Illustration 17*).

1. Cut off the heads of a bunch of Yellow stamens and tape them to a 26 gauge wire

2. Roll out Pale Mauve flowerpaste and cut out 1-N1 six petal flower.
Place each petal over your finger and widen at the base with the petal veining tool (OP2) by rolling from the centre to the side, each way. Soften the edges with the balling tool (OP1). Make a ridge down the centre of each petal with tweezers.

3. Brush a little glue onto the base of the stamens and thread the wire through the centre of the flower. Pop into the flowerstand (S1) and prop the petals with 'cloud drift'. Leave to dry. (See Illustration 18).

4. When dry, dust with Burgundy colour petal dust.

5. Buds. The bud is a very pointed cone of Green paste pushed onto the glued end of a 26 gauge wire. Mark the vertical grooves with a palette knife. As they get bigger, cut into the cone to simulate closely wrapped petals.

6. Leaves. Roll out a pointed cone of Pale Green paste, flatten and mark the veins with the petal veining tool (OP2), or make a leaf mould from Milliput, as in Book 2.

19

20

Tobacco Plant (*See Illustration 19*).

1. Tape 5 Claret coloured stamens and 1 stamen (piston) to the end of a 26 gauge wire. The piston should protrude above the stamens.

2. Make a 'Mexican Hat' of White paste (as described on Page 2) and cut out 1-R11A

Calyx. Push the veining tool (OP2) into the centre and pressing hard vein the petals from side to side to widen. Apply a little glue to the base of the stamens and thread through the centre of the flower. Leave to dry. (See Illustration 20). When dry dust the centre vein pink and the edges and back of the flower pink. Paint a green calyx onto the base and dust pale green and yellow up the base.

Buds. Green cone on a glued 24 gauge wire, elongate the top and cut into 4 sections. Pinch around the cone with a pair of tweezers to create grooves. When dry, dust a darker shade of green in the grooves.

21

22

Snowdrop (*See Illustration 21*).

1. Moisten the end of a 33 gauge wire and push on a tiny ball of Yellow paste.

2. Roll out White paste and cut out 1-Daphne (D1). Cut off one petal. Cut out a little triangle at the end of each remaining petal with R4 (petal cutter). Place on the Orchard Pad (PD1) and ball each of the petals from the outside to the centre.

Place on a soft sponge and cup by pressing in the centre with the balling tool (OP1).

3. Moisten the base of the Yellow paste with rose water and thread the wire through the centre of the flower. Cup the petals round the ball of paste. Leave to dry.

4. Paint Dark Green zigzag lines onto the petal just a little way up from the base. Leave to dry in the smallest hole in the flower stand (S1).

5. Roll out White flowerpaste and cut out 1-R12 (Calyx). Cut off two of the petals and cut off the tips of the remaining petals with the straight blade from the Endless Garrett Frill cutter (EGF6). (See Illustration 22).

6. Turn the paste over onto the pad and vein with the petal veining tool (OP2). Turn it back again and ball each petal from the outside to the centre.

7. Brush a little glue onto the base of the inside petals -'daphne'- and wrap the 'calyx' petals around, interleaving them. Leave to dry.

8. When dry, apply glue to the base of the snowdrop and thread a small Green ball of paste onto the wire. Gently squeeze with your fingers to mould around the base of the flower.

9. Tape a small piece of Green florists tape, with a rounded end cut down the centre, to the top of the flower.

23

Bride and Groom Wedding Cake (*See Illustrations 23, 29 & Template 26*).

Note: Read these instructions through before starting and plan your work to avoid wasting too much time waiting for things to dry. The cake should be 10" dia.

1. The 14" cake board is covered with one layer of satin and an overlay of tulle material as described in Book 5 'Great Ideas for Cake Decorators' Page 22.

2. Roll out pastillage and cut out 1- 6" dia. circular plaque and a P3 plaque. A 6" cake board can be used as a template for the circle. Cut off a segment about 1" deep from the circle.

Trim the P3 to make a near right-angled corner as the Template 24. This will act as a rear support for the plaque *. Leave on a cornflour dusted board to dry.

Dust the background on the plaque with Pale Blue petal dust. Rub it over with a tissue to obtain a smooth look.

When dry, trace the outline of the drawing onto the plaque, just the back of the heads, not the faces.

Alternatively you could use a segment of cake to support the plaque, hollowed out, with a battery light concealed in it!

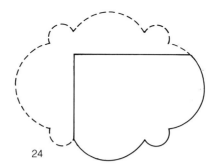

24

3. Make a photocopy of Template 26. Pop the drawing of the design into a clear plastic folder. This is to protect the drawing, prevent it from smudging, and makes it easier to get the sugarpaste off.

4. The face. See Illustration 27. For the cheeks roll a small pea sized ball of sugarpaste, place it onto the drawing where the cheek is (on top of the plastic), and gently stroke out the sides with your forefinger until it reaches the row of dots.

For the forehead, make a sausage of sugarpaste and taper at both ends. Place in between the dotted forehead lines and proceed as above. When complete, brush a little rose water onto the plaque and transfer the sections onto their correct positions on the plaque with an artists palette knife. This technique is described in detail in Book 4 'Creative Ideas for Cake Decorators' Page 31 onwards.

5. Roll out Flesh coloured sugarpaste and cut out 1- Face (HD2). Pop the face over the modelling pieces, and gently stroke down with your forefinger starting at the cheek until the face is in position. Indent the neck so that it lies underneath the head.

When dry, dust the cheek and forehead with light Skintone or Pale Pink petal dust. Paint the eye, the eyebrow and the lips using a very fine (000) sable paintbrush. The eyes are Brown and the lips Pale Pink plus a spot of Brown for the man.

6. With the Bride looking right, turn the face (HD2) over before proceeding as above.

7. Groom's Ear. Make a tiny ball of Flesh-toned sugarpaste, pop onto the head with rosewater, and indent with the end of a paintbrush allowing for a thicker outer rim. Dust the outer rim with Light Skintone or similar.

8. Hair. Pipe with Pale Yellow Royal Icing in a piping bag without a tube. (The icing should be of 'peak' consistency, that is it stands up in 'peaks' when drawn out). Cut a very small hole in the end of the piping bag to represent a No.0 tube. Pipe any strands of hair or fringes. Gently stroke the strands downwards using a fine (00) sable paintbrush. The paintbrush should be slightly dampened i.e. put the brush in the water and squeeze the excess out between your finger and thumb.

Leave the back of the bride's hair until the dress is completed, since the hair comes over the dress.

The groom's hair should be Dark Brown or Black.

9. Shoe. Fashion a small shoe out of sugarpaste following the pattern on the drawing by cutting round it. Attach to the plaque with rose water.

10. Groom's body. Roll out Pale Mauve sugarpaste or flowerpaste and cut to shape following the outline. Attach with rose water.
Use White sugarpaste for the collar.

11. Bride's dress. Make the plaque portion out of rolled White sugarpaste and indent the creases with the balling tool (OP1). Shape and leave to dry.

12. Arm. Roll out one long sausage of sugarpaste. Indent for the elbow and for the wrist. Glue into position with a little rose water.

13. Groom's Hand. Roll out a sausage of Skintone paste tapered at one end, flatten the tapered end with the side of your little finger. Cut out a V shape with scissors to form the thumb, then make only 3 more cuts to make 4 fingers. (4 cuts makes 5 fingers and 1 thumb!)

14. Pipe on the rest of the bride's hair, and while it is still wet, pop on a couple of roses. Leave the whole thing to dry.

15. When thoroughly dry, attach the P3 support to the back of the plaque with Royal Icing, so that it stands up. Place in position on the cake. (See Illustration 25).

16. Roll out White flowerpaste and cut out the remainder of the bride's dress to Template 26. Drape into position while still soft and leave to dry.

17. Veil. Cut out a triangular shape from tulle, gather the top together, bend it over and attach to the bride's hair with a little gum glue. Leave this to dry thoroughly before arranging the veil.
Drape the veil around the figure and down to the bottom of the cake and trim to length. Then pipe small dots of Royal Icing over it with a 00 tube. Put tiny blossoms on the top of the veil.

18. To finish off, cut a strip of narrow paper ribbon and wrap it round the top of the plaque, fixing with gum glue. Add a few little flowers at the side.

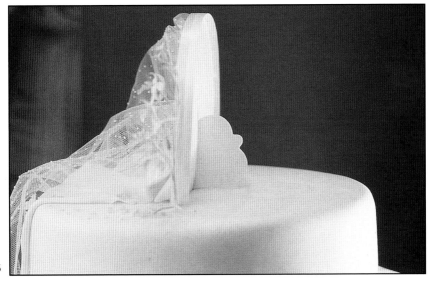

25

28

29

Bridesmaids. (*See Illustration 29*).

General Note: It is easier if you work on the two figures together.

1. Roll out pastillage and cut out the outline of each bridesmaid. Leave to dry thoroughly. (Full details of how to make bas-relief figures are given in Book 4 'Creative Ideas for Cake Decorators' Page 30).

2. Face. For the cheeks roll a pea sized ball of sugarpaste and place it on the cheek on the drawing on top of the plastic, and gently stroke out the sides with your forefinger until it spreads out to the row of dots.

For the forehead, make a sausage of paste tapered at both ends, place in the middle of the dotted forehead lines and repeat as above.

When complete, brush a little rose water onto the shape in Step 1, and, using an artist's palette knife, transfer the modelling sections to their correct positions on the plaque.

3. Roll out Flesh coloured sugarpaste and cut out 1-HD1 (Face).

(For the face looking left, turn the piece over).

Place onto the Orchard Pad (PD1) and gently smooth the front of the face and neck with your little finger to eliminate the 'cut' look. Pop the face cutout over the modelling piece and smooth gently down with your forefinger, starting with the cheek, until the face is in position.

Indent the neck so that it lies underneath the head. When dry, dust the cheek and forehead with light Skintone or Pale Pink petal dust.

4. Dress. Roll out flowerpaste mixed with sugarpaste and cut out the dress following the drawing 29. Make it a little wider each side to allow for the folds. Brush a little rose water or paste glue onto the outline of the figure and pop the dress on so that the material completely hides the outline. To make the folds, push a couple of paintbrush handles under the dress and stroke the folds in with the balling tool (OP1). Leave to dry.

5. Base of Dress. Cut out 1 strip with the Endless Garrett Frill cutter assembly EGF5 and EGF8. Frill with a Frilling Tool (FT1 - 4). Attach to the bottom of the dress with a little rose water. REMEMBER the figure has to - stand up, so do not place the frill below the base line.

6. Arm. Roll a small sausage of Pink coloured paste for the arm. For the sleeve, roll out the pattern wider than the drawing and fold round the arm. Stick down with rose water.

7. Hands. Roll out a sausage of Skintone sugarpaste tapered at one end. Flatten the tapered end with the outside of your little finger. Cut out a V shape for the thumb with a pair of very fine scissors, and then make 3 more cuts for 4 fingers. Stick in position on the ends of the arms with rose water.

8. Cuff. Cut a small strip of paste, frill the edges and wrap round the end of the sleeve, sticking with rose water.

9. Collar. Cut a narrow strip of paste with the straight blade of the Endless Garrett Frill cutter (EGF6) and frill. Stick round the neck with rose water.

10. Hair. Pipe the hair with Yellow Royal Icing in an icing bag with a size '0' hole cut in the end.

11. Attach to the side of the cake at the head with tacky paste glue.

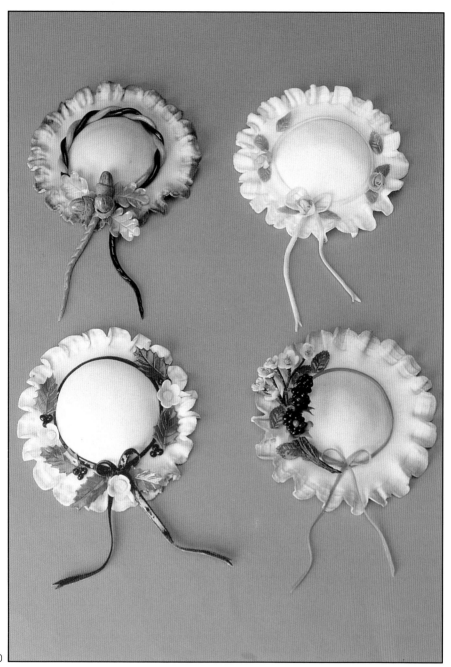

30

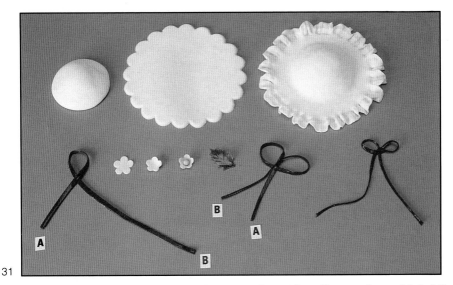

Ladies Hat - Favours for weddings or fêtes (*See Illustrations 30 & 32*).

1. Roll out a ball of sugarpaste to fit cutter GF2 (Garrett Frill set) and flatten the top. When dry dust liberally with cornflour.

2. Cut out 1-GF1 and frill the edges with a Frilling tool (FT1-4). Place on top of the flattened ball and shape. Leave to dry. Then, if you wish to fill the hat with sugared almonds, remove the centre ball. Pop in the almonds, cut out another GF1, frill the edges and glue lightly to the underside of the hat, so that it can be removed.

3. Bow. Roll out flowerpaste and cut out a narrow strip about 4mm ($^1/_8$") wide with the EGF6 blade. Lay it on the board and position it to make a little triangle. Wrap the first loop over the top and then you have ends A & B, as in Illustration 31.

4. Take strip B, form another loop and cross it over so that it goes to the left side of A. See also Illustration 33.

32

33

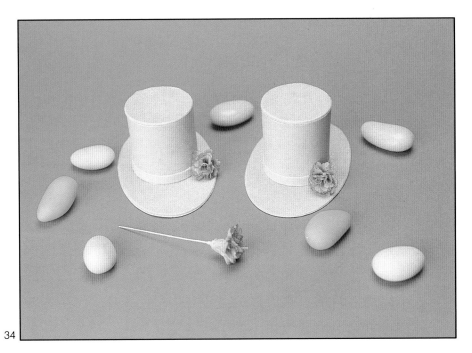

Top Hat-Favours for weddings or fêtes (See Illustration 34).

1. Roll out Grey pastillage and cut out 1 oval shape (8cm) 3$\frac{1}{4}$" long as the template 35. Leave to dry. Roll out Grey pastillage and cut out a circle (3cm) 1$\frac{1}{4}$" diameter for the top. Leave to dry.

2. Roll out Grey pastillage and cut out a rectangle* (3cm x 10cm) 1$\frac{1}{4}$"x 4". The straight blade of the Endless Garrett Frill cutter (EGF6) is a very useful tool for this purpose as it does not 'drag' the paste.

3. Dust the outside of an empty 35mm film container with cornflour and wrap the rectangle of paste round the container. When dry, remove from the container and stick to the oval base with Royal Icing or with the Grey pastillage softened with water. Mash it down with a palette knife until it becomes 'gluey'. Smooth the join with this glue. (See Illustration 36).

Put plenty around the circle and just before it dries smooth the outside join with a palette knife. Fill with sugared almonds.

The top is intended to be used as a lid, so only use a small quantity of paste on opposite sides to stick it, so that it can be removed easily with a knife.

4. Roll out very Pale Grey flowerpaste and cut out a ribbon with the EGF6 blade and wrap round the base of the hat. Stick with a litte rose water. Leave to dry. Dust with Silver Sparkle.

5. To finish off, make a small carnation (Book 3) and lay it at the side.

It is quicker to use a permanent template for the rectangle made from an ice cream container.

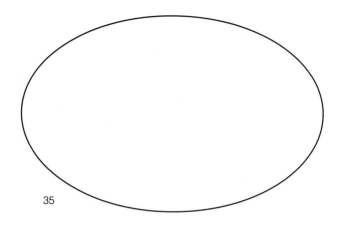

35

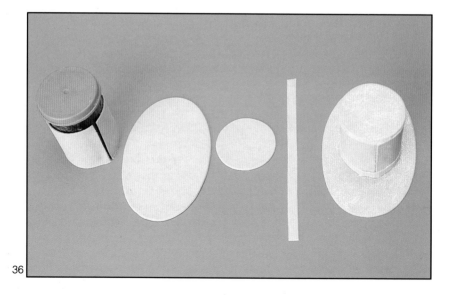

36

37

Acorn (*See Illustration 37*).

1. Shell. Roll a ball of Fawn coloured paste. Push the small end of the balling tool (OP1) well in to form a cap and, holding it on the balling tool, make little indentations with a cocktail stick. Leave to dry.

To make a wired acorn, hook a 28 gauge wire, moisten with rose water and push through the base of the shell while still soft.

2. Acorn. Roll a cone shape of Light Browny/Yellow paste. Moisten the base with rosewater and pop it into the shell.

Oak Leaves. See Book 5 'Great Ideas for Cake Decorators' Page 38.

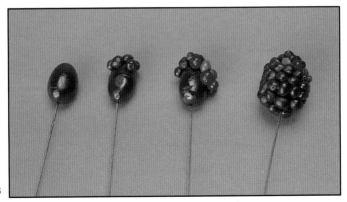

38

Blackberries (*See Illustration 38*).

1. Shape a rounded cone of Black flowerpaste. Roll out small balls of Black, Red and Green flowerpaste and attach them onto the cone with rose water or paste glue.

2. Calyx. Roll out Green paste and cut out 1- R15 Small calyx. Glue the base of the blackberry and press the calyx on.

When dry, paint over the top with confectioners glaze.

39

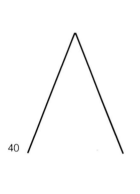

40

41

Nameplates. (*See Illustration 39*).

This idea came from Jean Rushbrooke (Sussex Branch BSG).

1. Roll out White pastillage and cut out 1-P3 Plaque. Bend a section of the plaque carefully over the corner of a cardboard triangle shaped to line up with the Diagram 40 and Illustration 41. Leave to dry.

2. Pipe the name on with Royal Icing in a piping bag with a No. 0 tube and decorate with small flowers or leaves attached·with a spot of Royal Icing.

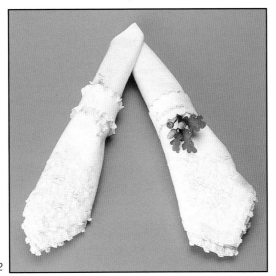

42

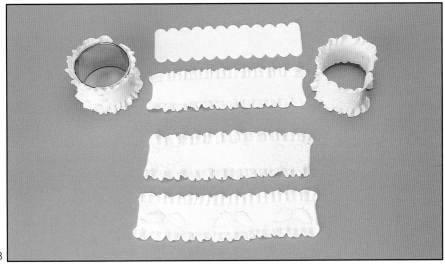

43

Serviette Rings. (*See Illustration 42*).

1. Cut out a strip of pastillage using the Endless Garrett Frill cutter (EGF5) and the Additional Blade (EGF8) fitted in the 'wide' position. Flute the sides with a Frilling Tool (FT1-4) and emboss each end and the middle with the Small Blossom cutter (F2S) or the Holly Leaf cutter (H4). (See Illustration 43).

2. Dust a serviette ring with cornflour and wrap the strip round. Leave to dry. When dry, dust the edges with petal dust and pipe the name with Royal Icing. Add a flower or leaf spray for decoration.

Holly Wreath. *(See illustration 44).*

1. The wreath illustrated is 3½" dia.

Roll out 2 pencil shape strips of Brown pastillage (or flowerpaste) about 10½" long and lay side by side. Twist the tops together. Hold up and wrap one 'pencil' round the other. Lay on a cornflour dusted board, form into a circle and leave to dry.

2. Decorate with Red ivy leaves (IV4), Green holly (H4), Red berries and mini Christmas roses. (See Illustration 45).

3. Christmas Rose. Roll out White flowerpaste and cut out several small blossoms (F2). Pop onto the flowerstand (S1) or soft sponge and press in the centre with the balling tool (OP1) to cup. Leave to dry.

4. When dry dust the centre Pale Green. Glue the centre and pop in a small ball of Yellow sugarpaste.

5. Cones. Form a Brown cone of flowerpaste. Hold the top of the cone between your finger and thumb, cut V shapes all the way round the bottom with a sharp pointed pair of scissors. Cut another layer of V's above the first and between the V's of the lower layer. Continue in this manner up to the top.

46

47

Montbretia (*See Illustration 46*).

1. Pistil. Cut off the 'head' of an Orange stamen, flatten and spread out the tip. Cut into 3 with scissors and spread out. Tape 3 Orange stamens onto the pistil. The pistil protrudes slightly above the stamens.

2. Make a Mexican Hat (as described on Page 2) and cut out 1-N3 six petal flower from Orange flowerpaste.

3. Hold the crown of the hat between your thumb and forefinger, lay a petal over your finger and widen and vein each petal with the petal veining tool (OP2) by putting the point of the tool at the base, and firmly rolling the tool from side to side.

Stroke a central vein with the single end of the veining tool (OP2). Place on the Orchard Pad (PD1) and soften the edges with the balling tool.

4. Make a recess in the centre of the flower with a cocktail stick. Glue the base of the stamens and thread through the centre of the flower, then taper the stem by rolling between your finger and thumb. Place in the flowerstand (S1) and leave to dry. (See Illustration 47).

Paint the base Green with Dark Orange markings at the base of three petals.

5. Leaves. Roll out a long pointed sausage from Green paste, flatten and stroke one central vein with the single end of the petal veining tool. Push the glued end of a 26 gauge wire into one end.

48

Edible Ribbon Insertion (*See Illustration 48*). *(This idea came from Betty Debnam of Tasmania based on Leslie Herbert's 'Edible Ribbon').*

1. Cut a $^1/_4$" wide strip of paste with the straight blade of the Endless Garrett Frill cutter (EGF6) and lay it along the fixed blade of the Cutter (EGF5) and/or the Additional blade EGF8.

Press it gently into the flutes and then cut across the strip at the high points with a pair of scissors. Leave to dry.

2. When dry, just push each section into the required position, first one side and then press in the other side, on the plaque or cake while still soft. The plaque shown in Illustrations 48 and 50 is P5 which has 24 flutes, and the two blades mentioned above together provide just enough ribbon pieces to go round.

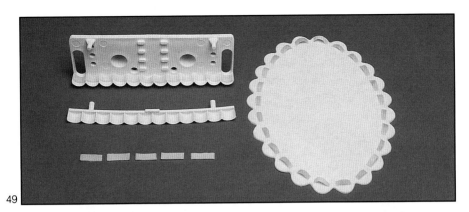

49

50

51

52

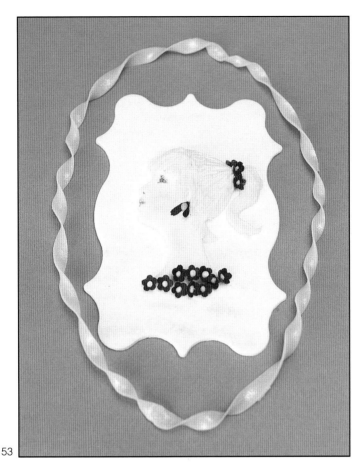

The Girl's Face (*See Illustrations 52 & 53*).

1. Roll out White pastillage and cut out 1- P4 plain oval plaque. Leave to dry.

2. Face (See Page 18 & illustration 27 on P.20). For the cheeks roll a pea sized ball of sugarpaste and place it on the cheek on the drawing on top of the plastic, and gently stroke out the sides with your forefinger until it spreads out to the row of dots.

the middle of the dotted forehead lines and repeat as above.

When complete, brush a little rose water onto the plaque in Step 1, and, using an artist's palette knife, transfer the modelling sections to their correct positions on the plaque.

3. Roll out Skintone sugarpaste and cut out 1-HD2 Lady's Face. Smooth down the edges with your forefinger.

Paint in the features with a sable '000' paint brush and edible colours.

4. Brush a little rose water onto the plaque and lay the HD2 face in position. Pipe the hair with Brown Royal Icing in an icing bag with a size '0' hole cut in the end.

5. Dress. Roll out sugarpaste and cut out several straight Garrett frills with the Endless Garrett Frill cutter EGF5/6.

Frill the edge and build up the layers of the dress, starting at the bottom, fixing them with a little rose water.

6. Ribbon. Roll out Pink flowerpaste and cut a ribbon 5mm wide and about 14" long with the straight blade of the Endless Garrett Frill cutter (EGF6). Twist it and lay in position. Stick with paste glue.

7. Small Flowers. Dip the end of a 33 gauge wire into rose water and push into a small ball of White flowerpaste.

Roll between finger and thumb to form a sausage shape and pull the sausage up until it just overhangs the end of the wire. Indent the tip of the sausage with the small end of the balling tool (OP1) to make a cup in the stem for the flower to sit in.

8. Roll out White flowerpaste and cut out 1-N8 six petal flower. Place on the Orchard Pad (PD1) and ball each petal from the outside in towards the centre with a very small balling tool or glass headed pin pushed into a piece of dowel. Transfer to a soft sponge and press in the centre to cup.

9. Moisten the base of the flower with rose water and press gently onto the indentation on top of the stem with the balling tool. Make sure the flower sits properly. Make a small indentation in the centre with the single end of the veining tool. Push in 4 or 5 Brown headed stamens.

10. When dry, dust the centre Blue, the outside of the petals Pink, and Pale Green down the stem.

11. Tape about a dozen flowers and buds together to form the spray.

RECIPES

Flowerpaste A. 250g (1lb) Bakels 'Pettinice' or Craigmillars 'Pastello' only.
1 teaspoon (5ml) Gum Tragacanth.
Rub 'Trex' on your hands and knead ingredients together until elastic. Wrap tightly in plastic and store in an airtight container. Leave for 24 hours. There is no need to refrigerate. This paste keeps well if worked through, say, once a week. Always keep tightly wrapped.

Flowerpaste D. 450g sieved icing sugar
5mls Gum Tragacanth and 20mls Carboxymethylcellulose (CMC)
10mls powdered Gelatine soaked in 25mls cold water
10mls white fat (Trex or Spry, not lard)
10mls liquid Glucose
45mls egg white

Sieve all the icing sugar into a greased* (Trex) mixing bowl. Add the gums to the sugar. Warm the mixture in a microwave oven 3 x 50 secs on a medium setting, stirring in between.

Sprinkle the gelatine over the water in a cup and allow to 'sponge'. Put the cup in hot,not boiling water,until clear. Add the white fat and liquid glucose. Heat the 'K' or Dough hook beater, add the dissolved ingredients and the egg white to the warmed sugar, and beat on the lowest speed until all the ingredients are combined. At this stage the mixture will be a dingy beige colour . Turn the machine to maximum speed and mix until the mixture becomes white and stringy. Grease your hands and remove the paste from the machine. Pull and stretch the paste several times. Knead together and cut into 4 sections. Knead each section again and place in a plastic bag, then in an airtight container and keep in the refrigerator. Let it mature for 24 hours. This paste dries very quickly so, when ready to use, cut off only a very small piece and re-seal the remainder. Work it well with your fingers. It should 'click' between your fingers when ready to use. If it should be a little too hard and crumbly, add a little egg white and fat. The fat slows down the drying process and the egg white makes it more pliable.

Keep coloured paste in separate container. This paste keeps for several months.

* This eases the strain on the machine considerably.

Royal Icing   450g (1lb) icing sugar
*10g (3 x 5ml teaspoons) Albumen (dried hen egg whites)
or approx. 3 egg whites
90ml (3 fluid ozs) tepid water

Add Albumen to water and whisk with a wire whisk. Place in a mixing bowl and gradually add the icing sugar. Mix until the consistency of unwhipped cream. Stir at this stage and continue adding the sugar and stirring until the desired consistency is obtained (cold meringue). If using a machine do not overbeat. Use a 'K' beater on the lowest speed.

To test, lift the icing with a spatula and it should be just capable of forming a peak and holding its shape on withdrawing the spatula slowly from the bowl. Scrape down the sides of the bowl and cover with a damp cloth. Otherwise a crust will form making the icing difficult to use.

*or in accordance with the manufacturers instructions, which may vary slightly from this recipe.

Gum Glue.

Gum glue can be made with either sugarpaste, flowerpaste or pastillage. Use small quantities. Mash down the paste with a pallette knife adding water until a 'gluey' consistency is achieved. Use at once.

Pastillage   500g icing sugar
10g Gelatine
30g Royal Icing
30g cornflour
60g water

Sprinkle the gelatine over the water in a cup and allow to 'sponge'. Put the cup into hot, not boiling water, until clear.

Sift the icing sugar and cornflour into a bowl. Pour the warm gelatine into the centre stirring with a knife, add the Royal Icing and knead until it forms a paste.

Wrap in clingfilm and pop into an airtight container. Leave for a few hours to mature. This paste will keep for several days.

Gum Arabic Glue.

Use proportions of 3:1 of tepid water and Gum Arabic, i.e. 3 teaspoons of water to 1 teaspoon of Gum Arabic. Place in a small glass bottle (say 15ml) with screw top and brush, or clean nail varnish container and shake well. This saves continually cleaning the brush, and keeps it moist.

3-D CITY GUIDES
MANHATTAN

3-D CITY GUIDES

MANHATTAN

THE ULTIMATE STREET-BY-STREET MAP AND GUIDE

Written by Fiona Duncan and Leonie Glass

Maps created by Irwin Technical

DUNCAN•PETERSEN

This edition published 1992 by Duncan Petersen Publishing Ltd

© Maps and text Duncan Petersen Publishing Ltd 1992

Conceived, edited and designed by
Duncan Petersen Publishing Ltd,
54, Milson Road,
London W14 OLB

Distributed in the United Kingdom and Ireland
by World Leisure Marketing Limited,
117 The Hollow, Littleover, Derby DE3 7BS, England

Filmset by SX Composing, Rayleigh, Essex
Printed by Mateu Cromo, Madrid, Spain.

Every reasonable care has been taken to ensure the information in this guide is accurate, but the publishers and copyright holders can accept no responsibility for the consequences of errors in the text or on the maps, especially those arising from closures, or those topographical changes occurring after completion of the aerial survey on which the maps are based.

ISBN 1-872576-15-X

ACKNOWLEDGEMENTS

The authors would like to thank the following people for their help and advice: Jai Singh; Peter Bejger; Nancy Batterman and Ricky Greenberg; Christopher McIntosh and Katharine Kurs; Louise Schneider.

Editorial

Editor	Fiona Duncan
Assistant editor	Kate Macdonald
Index	Rosemary Dawe

Design

Art director	Mel Petersen
Designers	Chris Foley and Beverley Stewart

Aerial survey by Skyviews Survey Inc., Ramsey, New Jersey
Maps created by Irwin Technical Ltd, 10-18, Clifton Street, London EC2A 4BT

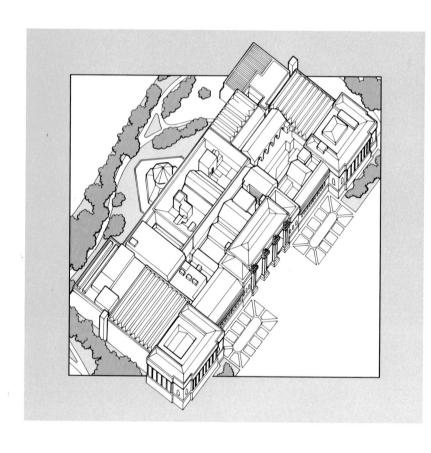

Contents

Acknowledgements 5

About this book 8-9

Master location maps 10-13

Essential information for
    visitors to Manhattan 14-25

New York Subway system 26-27

THE ISOMETRIC MAPS 28-131

Index of points of interest 132-138
    described in text

Index of people of interest 139-140
    described in text

Index of street names 141-144

About this book

How the mapping was made

Isometric mapping is produced from aerial photographic surveys. One was specially commissioned for 3-D Manhattan. The helicopter flew at about 1,500 feet, with the camera angled at 45°. Weather conditions had to be slightly overcast in order to achieve maximum detail on the buildings.

Scores of enlargements were made from the negatives, which Irwin Technical, a group of technical illustrators in London (address on page 5), then used to create the maps. It took well over 1,000 hours to complete the task.

'Isometric' projection means that verticals are the same height, whether in the foreground or the background – at the 'front' (bottom) of the page or at the 'back' (top). Thus the diminishing effect of perspective is avoided and all the buildings, whether near or distant, are shown in similar detail and appear at an appropriate height.

The order of the maps

The map squares are arranged in sequence running from north to south and from west to east. For further details, see the master location maps on pages 10-13.

Numerals on maps

Each numeral on a map cross refers to the text printed down the right hand border of the map. The numbers generally read from the top left of each map to the bottom right, in a west-east direction. However, there are deviations from this pattern when several interesting features occur close together, or within one street.

Opening and closing times

If a museum, display or exhibition is open during regular working hours, opening and closing times are not mentioned in the text accompanying the maps. Brief details are however given when opening times are irregular. In the case of historic or otherwise interesting buildings, assume that you cannot gain access to the interior unless opening times are mentioned.

Prices

Restaurants

$ means one person can eat for less than $25.
$$ means one person can eat for $25-60.
$$$ means one person generally pays more than $60.
Wine is not included.

Hotels

$ means the price per person per night is less than $125.

$$ means the price per person per night is $125-150.

$$$ means the price per person per night is more than $150.

Coverage

Manhattan is a machine, fuelled by the millions of people who pour through its streets and subways each day, many of them locked into an exhausting but addictive life style which makes anywhere else seem dull and slow. These days, the machine is in dire need of repair, but the sheer energy – and, if you are in the mood – the romance of the place is still undeniable. No guide book can cover everything of interest in Manhattan. This one contains a particularly wide range of information, and the writers concentrated on aspects of the city brought out by the special nature of the mapping, with emphasis on historical or general information that helped explain the fabric, evolution and working of the city. They have also tended to draw attention to the outstanding, even the peculiar, sometimes at the expense of the obvious and well-established, in the belief that this best reveals the essential character of a city. There is, in addition, much about eating, drinking, shopping and other practical matters.

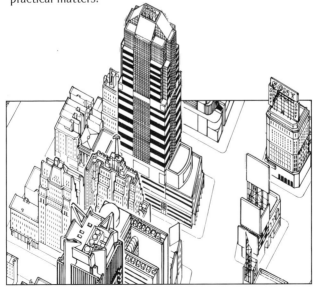

Master Location Map

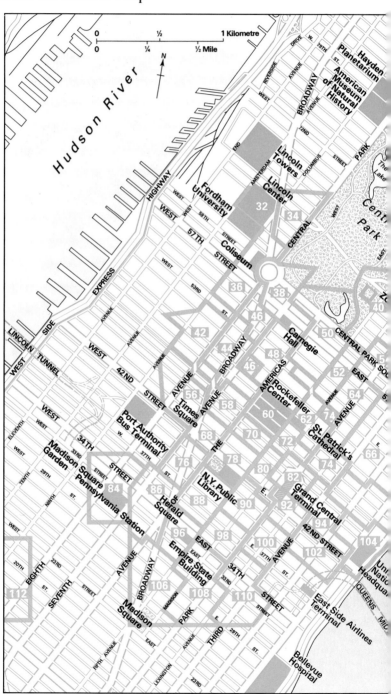

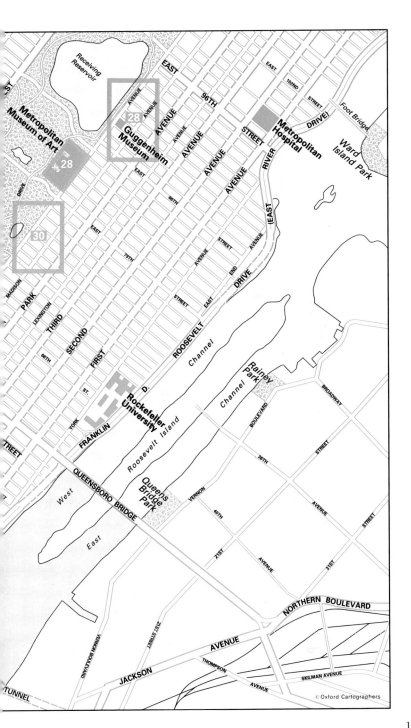

Master Location Map

Transport

From airports to city

The main gateway to North America, New York has three airports. Most transatlantic flights and many domestic services arrive and depart from John F. Kennedy International Airport in the borough of Queens, 15 miles (an hour's drive or $30-$35 taxi ride) from central Manhattan. All terminals are linked to the subway system by a frequent, free shuttle bus service.

Carey Transportation Inc. operate an express coach service to several Midtown locations including Grand Central Station and the Port Authority Bus Terminal every 30 minutes from 6 am to midnight. The Gray Line Air Shuttle (tel. 757 6840) shared minibus service runs from 7 am to 11 am with pick-up and drop-off points at major Manhattan hotels on request. There is a shared taxi scheme into Manhattan operating at a discount during peak hours.

Car drivers should take the Van Wyck Expressway on to Grand Central Parkway and connect with the Long Island Expressway (LIE). Exit the LIE via the Brooklyn Queens Expressway for destinations in Brooklyn and downtown Manhattan; continue on the LIE for Midtown.

La Guardia Airport in Queens, about 8 miles (a 30-minute drive or $20-$25 taxi ride) from Midtown, handles domestic air services and offers a similar free shuttle bus connection to the subway; an express coach link and a shared minibus scheme to the city. Drivers should follow directions for Grand Central Parkway to the Triborough Bridge (toll), or exit south

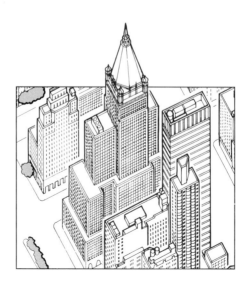

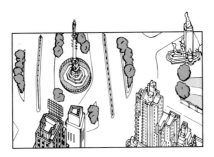

short of the bridge for the Queensborough Bridge connecting with Manhattan.

New York's second international airport, Newark, is one of the country's most up-to-date facilities. It is located in New Jersey, 16 miles (a 45-minute drive or $30 taxi ride) from Midtown. New Jersey Transit operate a 24-hour express coach service between all terminals and the Port Authority Bus Terminal in Manhattan. Olympia Trails run buses from the airport to Newark's Penn Station, Grand Central Station (every 20 minutes 6.15 am to midnight), and World Trade Center 1 (every 20-30 minutes 6 am to 10 pm). Airlink buses connect terminals with Pennsylvania Station; plus a shared minibus scheme operates to Manhattan hotels. Drivers follow the New Jersey Turnpike, and take the Holland Tunnel for Downtown destinations; or the Lincoln Tunnel for Midtown.

For travel information about airport journeys, call 800-AIRPORT.

City orientation

New York City is a conglomeration of five boroughs - Brooklyn, The Bronx, Queens, Staten Island and Manhattan. Manhattan Island is the heart of the City, just 13 miles long and two miles across at its widest point. Getting around is simplified by the grid pattern street plan with avenues running north to south, and cross streets running east to west. The exception is diagonal Broadway, also the Downtown district established before the grid system was imposed around 1811.

Traffic flow is generally one-way within the Midtown area; north-bound avenues are First, Third, Madison, Avenue of the Americas (Sixth), Eighth and Tenth; southbound traffic uses Second, Lexington, Fifth, Seventh, Ninth and Broadway; plus two-way traffic on York, Park, Eleventh and Twelfth.

Fifth Avenue marks the division between east and west cross-streets. The numbering of buildings begins at Fifth Avenue and mounts to the mid-hundreds to the east, and in the same way to the west. Even-numbered buildings are on the south side of cross-streets, odd-numbered on the north side.

Buses

The city's 3,600 buses serve 220 local and express routes throughout the boroughs. They are slow, particularly during peak periods, but you can see where you are going and over 80 per cent of them are thoughtfully equipped with wheelchair lifts. Destinations and route numbers are displayed on electronic signs at the front of the bus, and some bus stops feature Guide-a-Ride bus route maps. There is a fixed rate fare of $1.15 regardless of distance travelled which must be paid with exact change or transport tokens available from the subway.

Buses run along all the avenues and major cross-streets. Passengers who need to use two connecting buses to make a single journey can request a free transfer on boarding. There are reduced services on most routes at night.

For further information, call New York City Transit Authority (tel. (718) 330 1234) around the clock.

Subway

For all its appalling reputation, the New York subway carries 3.7 million passengers per day and remains the most efficient means of moving around the city.

The subway map appears brighter and more confusing than the most extravagant graffiti at first glance, but in general main subway lines run north-south beneath the avenues, and stations are named after cross-streets along the route. When you enter the subway, take the correct entrance for Uptown or Downtown locations.

There are two types of trains: Locals which serve every station; and Expresses which offer a swift alternative, stopping at specified main stations only. Signs on each subway car give details of route, point of origin and destination.

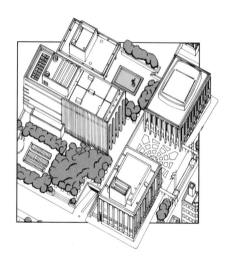

The $1.15 flat rate fare is paid by tokens available individually or in packs of ten (no discount) from token booths, and fed into the turnstile. Trains run 24 hours a day, with reduced services at night, and limited daytime routes in some cases.

It is best to arm yourself with a New York City Transit Authority map available at token booths and from the Tourist Office, as maps within the subway system are hard to find. Try not to look too much of a tourist, carry insecure bags or wear flashy jewellery. The subway is not a wise place to wait around in the evening. There are off-peak waiting areas by the token booths.

Taxis

There are 12,000 licensed yellow taxis in New York City, and none appear to pick up fares in the rain. There is also a growing number of so-called 'gypsy' cabs which are generally owner-operated, unlicensed and to be avoided except *in extremis*. Ordinary yellow cabs can accept four passengers; the old Checker cabs are licensed for up to five persons. If a cab is available for hire it will display a yellow light on the roof; the driver must activate the meter immediately.

Passengers are liable for any bridge or tunnel tolls incurred, but fares are reasonable; however they rise dramatically after 8 pm and on Sundays. Also beware the price hike the moment you move outside the New York City limits: for Newark Airport add $10 to the metered amount; for Westchester and Nassau counties you will pay double the metered amount for the portion of the trip outside the city limits.

It is worth checking out your route before you pick up a cab, and keep a map handy. A large proportion of New York cabbies are recent immigrants with a somewhat loose grasp of city geography, and a looser command of the language. There is no harm in clarifying your instructions with the aid of a map. Cabbies expect a tip in the region of 15 per cent, or round up the fare to the nearest dollar.

If you have a complaint about a yellow cab, take the identification number from the taxi receipt or dashboard, and call 221 8294. To report lost property, call 840 4734.

Private cars

Driving is not a recommended pastime for visitors, and parking is a nightmare. Parking lots in Manhattan are wildly expensive, and the limited street parking is governed by a series of fiendish regulations such as parking on alternate sides of the street on alternate days, or even for certain hours within the day. There are confusing signs (including one which reads 'Don't Even THINK of Parking Here'); color-coded pavement markings; no parking in front of fire hydrants; and a tow-away fine of around $100 plus a wasted day. Front seat belts are compulsory; there is a 35mph speed limit; and breathalyzer tests for drink-drivers. Don't overtake a stopped schoolbus with flashing lights either, it is illegal and warrants a heavy fine. If this does not convince you, take a cab ride and imagine how you would feel if the driver was not on your side.

Beyond the city

By train New York City is served by two main railroad stations, both located in Manhattan: Grand Central Station, 42nd Street and Park Avenue (tel. 532 4900); and Pennsylvania (Penn) Station, West 34th Street, between Seventh and Eighth Avenues (tel. 582 6875). Northern commuter line services from the Hudson Valley and New Haven arrive at Grand Central; while eastern line services from Long Island and New Jersey use Pennsylvania Station. Long-distance Amtrak services from Boston, Canada, Chicago, Florida, Washington and the West can arrive and depart from either station. For details, contact Amtrak-National Railroad Passenger Corp., 1 Penn Plaza, Suite 1435 (information tel. 800 872 7245).

By air As the major international gateway to North America, New York is also a prime domestic destination with all three airports handling domestic flights. There are frequent shuttle services to Boston and Washington DC, and a comprehensive network of short- and long-haul flights to other parts

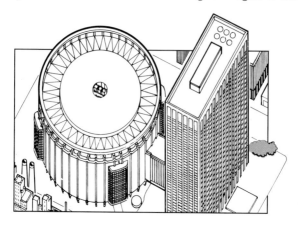

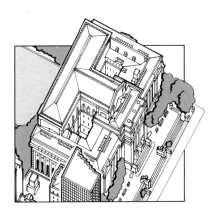

of the country. Major carriers (including American, Delta, USAir, North-west, Pan Am, TWA and United) advertize in the local press, and it is worth checking for discounts available on low season and off-peak services like the late night 'red eye' flights. Tickets can be booked direct through the air-lines and picked up at the airport, or purchased through the Airlines Ticket Office, 100 East 42nd Street (tel. 986 0888).

By bus Bussing around the States is not the great deal is used to be. Low-priced airline tickets have considerably reduced the number of passengers prepared to sit it out on the road, and bus services have been cut back. For details of nationwide bus services, contact Greyhound Trailways (informa-tion tel. 564 8484). All bus services operate from New York City's Port Authority Bus Terminal, Eighth Avenue and West 43rd Street. Open 24 hours daily, it is not a good place to hang around at any time, and be parti-cularly careful at night.

By car The national inter-state and highway road network is subject to an overall 55mph speed limit, with a few rural exceptions where the limit is raised to 65mph. Traffic in built-up areas is restricted to 35mph. Minimum age limits and other regulations can differ from state to state, but it is almost impossible to hire a car under the age of 25 anywhere. Foreign licenses are valid for a period of one year, though it is advisable to apply for an International Driving Licence if you plan to travel extensively, and all documents must be in the car at all times.

Rand McNally publish the best route maps, and they are readily available from gas stations. Petrol sells by the US gallon (3.8 litres), slightly less than the Imperial gallon. The American Automobile Association, Broadway and 62nd Street (tel. 586 1166) offers useful reciprocal benefits to members of foreign national automobile associations. Contact them for details of free information and their excellent travel advisory service.

Useful data

Tourist information

For information before you go, the New York Convention and Visitors Bureau, and State of New York Division of Tourism have representative offices in several major overseas cities. In New York, you can find a wealth of free consumer literature, maps and guides at their Manhattan addresses:

■ New York Convention and Visitors Bureau, 2 Columbus Circle, West 59th Street and Broadway (tel. 397 8200); open 9 am to 6 pm Mon-Fri, 10 am to 6 pm Sat-Sun.

■ State of New York Division of Tourism, 1515 Broadway, 51st floor (tel. 827 6250); open 9 am to 5 pm Mon-Fri.

Disabled visitors can obtain specific information about facilities in New York from the Center for the Handicapped, Office 206, 52 Chamber Street (tel. 566 3913).

Bed and breakfast

A fast-growing concept in the US, bed and breakfast American-style is not the bargain accommodation found in the UK. Budget hotels are definitely cheaper, but within the middle range B&B is a welcome alternative to soul-less hotel rooms and can provide visitors with airport collection, a built-in advice and guide service, laundry facilities, a slap-up breakfast and, occasionally, friends for life. If you prefer, you can do without the breakfast and rent a self-contained privately-owned apartment. Several agencies provide information and reservations, including: B&B in the Big Apple, Box 426, New York 10024 (tel. 594 5650); and The B&B Group (New Yorkers at Home), 301 60th Street, New York 10022 (tel. 838 7015). In the UK, a free telephone call (tel. 0800 891696) will connect you direct to New World Bed and Breakfast, Suite 711, 150 Fifth Avenue, New York, NY 10011. London-based B&B operations include: Best Bed and Breakfast in the World (tel. 071 376 5051); Home Base Holidays (tel. 081 886 8752); and Welcome Homes (tel. 081 853 2706).

Sightseeing tours

New York has something for everyone and every imaginable type of sight-seeing opportunity has been spotted and neatly packaged by someone. You can take a spiritual walking tour of Harlem; make a helicopter circuit of Manhattan; clatter around Staten Island on a trolley bus; or sail the 70-foot 1938 Sparkman & Stephens racing yacht *Petrel* out into the Hudson River from Battery Park. On a more prosaic level, there are a host of bus tour operators and multi-lingual guide services listed among the 125 entries in the New York Convention and Visitors Bureau *Big Apple Guide*, including:

■ Gray Line New York Tours Inc., 254 West 54th Street; tel. 397 2620.

■ Short Line Tours, 166 West 46th Street; tel. 354 4740.

Boat trips The Circle Line Ferry offers a three-hour voyage around Manhattan Island daily March to December from Pier 83, west end of 42nd Street (information tel. 563 3200). Also a daily cruise to the Statue of Liberty and Ellis Island. For a bargain shipboard view of the Downtown skyline, nothing beats the 25c 45-minute Staten Island Ferry route.

Helicopter tours If you have a head for heights, this is the way to go. Short flights are reasonably priced, though you can wait an unreasonably long time in the line (queue) (no reservations) during peak season. There are two main operators:
- Island Helicopter Sightseeing, East 34th Street Heliport; tel. 683 4547.
- Manhattan Helicopter Tours, West 30th Street and Twelfth Avenue; tel. 247 8687.

Walking tours The following organizations offer a variety of city walking tours. Call ahead for details of schedules and departure points:
- Central Park (Urban Rangers); tel. 860 1353.
- Lower East Side Walking Tours and Living History Museum; tel. 431 0233.
- Museum of the City of New York; tel. 534 1672.
- 92nd Street Y Tours; tel. 996 1110.

Private guided tours For individual and group tours, contact:
- Guide Service of New York; tel. 408 3332.
- Guides Association of New York City; tel. 242 3900.

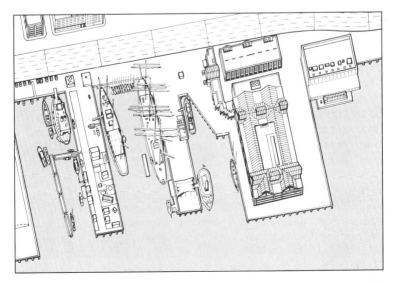

Shopping, banking and business hours

Midtown shops and stores are generally open 9 or 10 am to 6 pm Mon-Sat, with several stores reopening on Sunday. Late night is Thursday until 8 or 9 pm. Within the districts, this varies somewhat with shops and boutiques in Greenwich Village and SoHo pulling up the blinds around noon and staying open late; the Lower East Side shuts up on Friday afternoons, but bustles on Sundays; and the Financial District takes the weekend off. Fast-food outlets and delis open in time to feed the morning office rush-hour crowds and often stay upon until late.

Banking hours are 9 am to 3 pm, though a few central locations stay open a little later on Friday afternoon. Many bank branches will not exchange foreign currency. Citibank has several currency exchange facilities. The People's Foreign Exchange, 104 East 40th Street, between Park and Lexington (open 9 am to 6 pm Mon-Fri, 10.30 am to 3 pm Sat) buys and sells currencies and cashes major travellers cheques.

Traditional business hours are 8 am to 5 pm Mon-Fri, with the morning rush-hour commencing around 8 am until 9 am, and in the evening 5 pm to 6.30 pm.

Public holidays

The following public holidays are observed in New York State: New Year's Day (1 January); Martin Luther King Day (third Mon in January); Abraham Lincoln's Birthday (12 February); George Washington's Birthday (third Mon in February); Memorial Day (third Mon in May); Independence Day (4 July); Labor Day (first Mon in September); Columbus Day (second Mon in October); Veterans' Day (11 November); Thanksgiving (third Thur in November); Christmas Day (25 December).

The post

Normal post office hours are 8 am to 5 pm Mon-Fri. Major offices open 8 am to noon Sat, and New York's main General Post Office (Eighth Avenue and 33rd Street) is open 24 hours Mon-Sat. The U.S. Mail offers an Express Mail Service, and general parcel delivery. However, United Parcel Service often offers a better (and swifter) deal on heavy items. When posting items for delivery within the US, the inclusion of a zip code speeds up the process quite considerably. Stamps can be purchased from vending machines, shops and supermarkets as well as the post office.

Telephones

Pay phones can be found on sidewalks, in drugstores, gas stations, transport terminals and hotel lobbies. (It is much cheaper to call from a pay phonoe than from an hotel room.) Pay phones only accept 25c, 10c and 5c coins, which is extremely irritating when making long-distance calls. Collect (reverse charge) calls are made through the operator (dial zero).

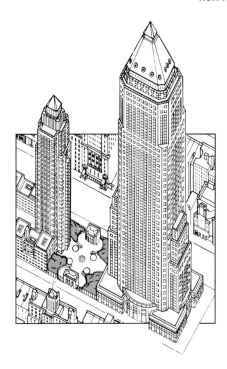

Within the U.S., telephone numbers come in three parts: the area code (three digits); the exchange code (three digits); and personal number (four digits). Within the same area, the initial three-digit code (i.e. 212 for New York City) is unnecessary. On most pay phones outside the area it is necessary to prefix the area code with 1 (i.e. 718 765 4321).

Insert the minimum fee (usually 25c) before dialling. Calls to the operator will be refunded. The most expensive time to call is 8 am to 5 pm; standard rate is 5 pm to 11 pm; cheap rate calls can be made between 11 pm and 8 am, and on weekends.

Some useful numbers:

■ For help from an operator dial 0 (zero). If you need an international operator, ask to be put through.

■ For directory enquiries in Manhattan and The Bronx dial 411; for Brooklyn, Queens and Staten Island dial 555 1212; for numbers outside New York, you must find the area code (i.e. 213 for Los Angeles), then dial 213 (the area code) 555 1212.

■ For international directory enquiries dial 00 (overseas operator).

■ For the speaking clock dial 976 1616.

■ For New York weather reports dial 976 1212.

■ In an emergency, dial 911 for police, fire and ambulance services. You will need a coin to call from a pay phone.

Publications

The *New York Times* is an institution with an excellent weekend section, published on Fridays, which lists current events alongside pithy reviews. Its tabloid rivals are the *New York Post* and *Daily News*. The latter boasts a better-than-average Sunday edition complete with good value *City Lights* listings supplement. *Village Voice* is the key to alternative entertainment in the Big Apple. Published on Thursdays, it covers all the mainstream events together with some truly bizarre happenings. The yuppified *New York Magazine*, and literary *New Yorker* also run a good check on what is on.

A couple of major bookstores are: B. Dalton, 666 Fifth Avenue; and Doubleday, 724 Fifth Avenue. For travel publications, there is The Complete Traveller, 199 Madison Avenue; the Rand McNally Bookstore, 10 East 53rd Street; The Traveller's Bookstore, 22 West 52nd Street; and the excellent New York Bound bookshop, in the lobby of The Association Press Building, 50 Rockerfeller Plaza. The New York Public Library is located at 42nd Street and Fifth Avenue.

Foreign consulates

- Australia 489 Fifth Avenue, 31st Floor, New York 10017 (tel. 687 6300).
- Canada 1251 Avenue of the Americas, New York 10020 (tel. 786 2400).
- France 972 Fifth Avenue, New York 10021 (tel. 439 1400).
- Germany 460 Park Avenue, New York 10022 (tel. 308 8700).
- Ireland 515 Madison Avenue, New York 10022 (tel. 319 2555).
- Italy 686 Park Avenue, New York 10021 (tel. 879 4242).
- Japan 299 Park Avenue, 16th Floor, New York 10171-0025 (tel. 371 8222).
- Netherlands One Rockefeller Plaza, 11th Floor, New York 10020 (tel. 246 1429).
- New Zealand 650 Fifth Avenue, Suite 530, New York 10111 (tel. 698 4650).
- Spain 2700 15th Street N.W., Washington D.C. 20008 (tel. (202) 483 4025).
- United Kingdom 845 Third Avenue, New York 10022 (tel. 752 5747).

Medical information

Hospitals

Private medical treatment in the U.S. is extremely expensive, but infinitely preferable to the public sector. Ensure that you are fully covered by travel insurance before you leave home.

Ambulances transport patients to the nearest municipal hospital.

There are 24-hour emergency departments at the following private hospitals: Cabrini Medical Center, 227 East 19th Street, tel. 995 6000; Mount

Sinai Hospital, Madison Avenue and West 100th Street, tel. 241 7171; New York Hospital, York Avenue and 70th Street, tel. 472 5454; New York University Medical Center, First Avenue and 30th Street, tel. 340 7300; Roosevelt Hospital, 428 West 59th Street and Ninth Avenue, tel. 523 4000; and St Vincent's Hospital, Seventh Avenue and West 11th Street, tel. 790 7997.

Late-night pharmacies

There is only one 24-hour pharmacy in Manhattan open daily: Kaufman's, 557 Lexington Avenue and East 50th Street, tel. 755 2266. Other late-night openers are: Plaza Pharmacy, 1657 Second Avenue and East 86th Street, tel. 879 3878 (until midnight daily); and Windsor Pharmacy, Sixth Avenue and West 58th Street, tel. 247 1538 (until 11.45 daily).

Doctors

Should you need to see a doctor during your stay, consult the Yellow Pages telephone directory, or visit one of the walk-in clinics, such as: Doctor's Walk-In, 57 East 34th Street, between Park and Madison Avenues, tel. 683 1010 (open 8 am to 6 pm Mon-Fri, 10 am to 2 pm Sat). For 24-hour house calls, contact Doctors House Call Service, tel. 1-718 436 9020. Both these services accept MasterCard (MC), Visa (V).

Clinics may expect a cash payment at the time of your visit. Make sure you have a receipt to be reimbursed by your insurers.

Dental treatment

Dentists are also listed in the Yellow Pages telephone directory. The New York University College of Dentistry operates a 24-hour hot-line daily (tel. 998 9872); and the Dental Emergency Service (tel. 679 3966 or 679 4172 after 8 pm) offers a 24-hour referral service. Be prepared to pay in cash, and secure a receipt.

Safety

Common sense is your best weapon on the streets of New York. An ogling tourist strung about with cameras, jewellery and a fat wallet of travellers cheques is bound to attract attention from unscrupulous elements. Just take what cash you need, dress casually and conceal valuables when possible. Look purposeful at all times, and keep to well-lit main streets by night, or better still catch a cab. Avoid dark alleys and doorways leading off the sidewalk. Kerb-crawlers are foiled if you walk against the traffic. Keep well clear of parks at night, and stick to the crowds and main paths during the day.

New York Subway system

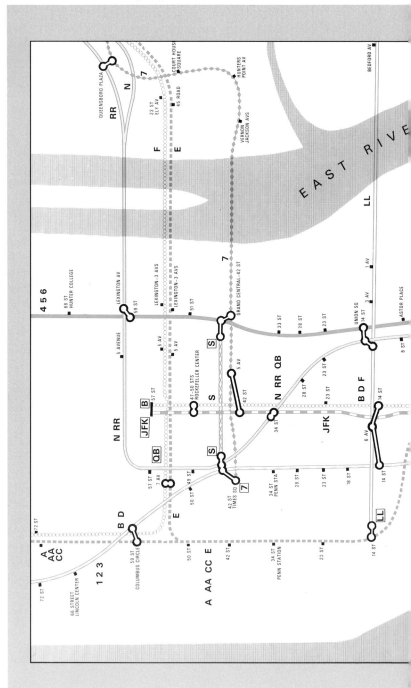

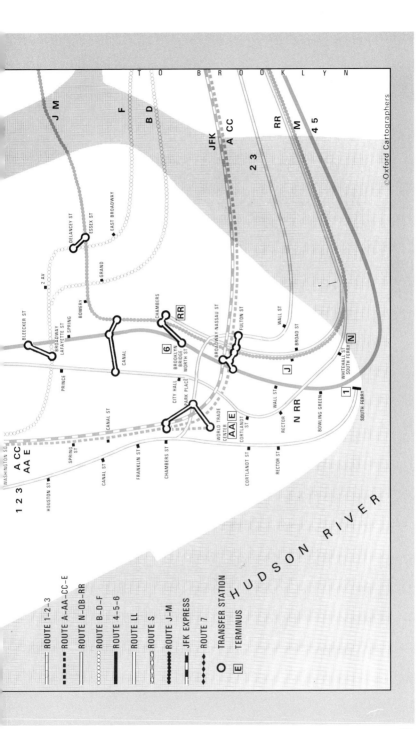

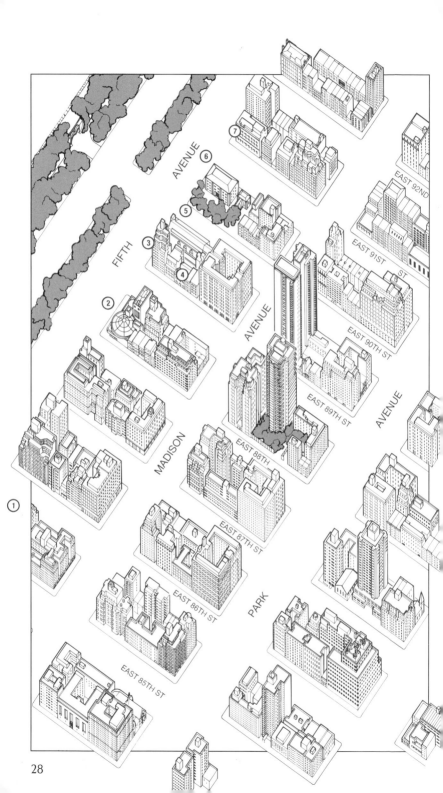

AVENUE

⑥

FIFTH

⑤

③

④

②

AVENUE

⑦

EAST 92ND

EAST 91ST
ST

EAST 90TH ST

EAST 89TH ST

AVENUE

MADISON

EAST 88TH

EAST 87TH ST

EAST 86TH ST

PARK

EAST 85TH ST

①

28

Upper East Side

Fifth Avenue's peerless mix of converted mansions and luxury apartment blocks, interspersed with museums, institutes and consulates, continues north as far as Carnegie Hill. Entrances are marked by smart awnings, often with the inevitable chauffeur-driven limousine waiting in front. ① A 1914 Carrère and Hastings mansion, modelled on a Louis XIII château, is today the **Yivo Institute For Jewish Research** (off map). ② Like it or not, the **Guggenheim**'s architecture overwhelms the art on its walls. Frank Lloyd Wright's only New York building (1959) evokes strong responses, but most agree that in is better than out. Take the elevator to the top, then wander down the spiral ramps taking in the permanent collection and temporary exhibitions of 20thC painting. The museum looks spick and span after its recent extensive renovation. ③ The **National Academy of Design**, together with its School of Fine Arts (5 E 89th St) holds the exhibitions of American, and occasionally European, art. ④ Notice next door (No. 9) the **New York Road Runners Club**, into which panting road runners disappear from time to time in varying degrees of collapse. Also in this street, **St David's** (Nos 12-16), where well-heeled WASPS send their children to school; around the corner, ⑤ the **Church of the Heavenly Rest**, where they worship. ⑥ With its wisteria-draped façade and alluring garden, the **Cooper-Hewitt Museum** comes as a breath of air, much like the Frick (*see page 31*). Andrew Carnegie, who built this mansion in 1901, was a friend of Frick's, and both were wealthy enough to award themselves the rare prize of a garden. A rich repository of the decorative arts, the collection was formed by Peter Cooper and his Hewitt grand-daughters. It is the New York branch of the Smithsonian Institute. ⑦ Three mansions on attractive 91st Street: No. 1, a private girls' school, **Convent of the Sacred Heart**, built in 1918 for Otto Kahn and apparently modelled on the Papal Chancellery in Rome; No. 7, the free-standing former **Burden House** (Warren and Wetmore, 1902) with a renowned spiral staircase; and No. 9, the former **Hammond House** (now the USSR consulate), Carrre and Hastings, 1906. The daughter of the house married Benny Goodman, who often played here in the 1930s.

EAST 79TH ST

EAST 78TH STREET

EAST 77TH STREET

AVENUE

EAST 76TH ST

FIFTH

EAST 75TH STREET

AVENUE

EAST 74TH

MADISON

AVE

EAST 73RD

PARK

EAST 72ND STREET

30

East Side at 72nd Street

Museum Mile starts here, with the ① **Frick Collection** (off map), which newcomers to New York will find the perfect restorative for whirring brains. The harmonious mansion of industrialist Henry Clay Frick, it is filled with exquisite European paintings and furniture. ② An exuberant Beaux Arts mansion now houses **Ralph Lauren** (off map), where the décor carefully reflects the preppy clothes. It is just one of hundreds of classy stores, antique shops and art galleries which make ③ **Madison Avenue** one of the world's most rarified shopping streets. ④ Two sensational townhouses, Nos 7 and 9, now house the **Lycée Français**. ⑤ A fine block: note **Nos 5**, **11**, **20**, **22** and **23**. ⑥ **Fraser Morris**, east-siders' favorite gourmet food store. ⑦ Looming alarmingly over the pavement, the **Whitney Museum of American Art** is an uncompromising Brutalist building (Marcel Breuer, 1966) with an uncompromising modern art collection. An invigorating contrast to the Frick. ⑧ Formerly **Harkness House** (1907), another palace-house, this with an iron fence topped with pineapples. ⑨ **Les Pleiades** (**$$$**), restaurant favored by the art world, and **Surrey Suite Hotel** (**$$$**). ⑩ The **Carlyle** has all the grandeur and panache of the great European hotels (**$$$**). ⑪ The **Mark** has panache too, and has established itself quickly as a haven for famous faces (**$$$**). A clutch of homes built for early millionaires: ⑫ former **James B. Duke residence**, modelled on a Bordeaux château (1912); ⑬ former **Payne Whitney residence**, McKim, Mead and White (1906); and ⑭ the **Ukranian Institute of America**, turreted French Gothic (1899). ⑮ **Metropolitan Museum of Art** (5th Ave. at 82nd St, inset). The largest repository of art in the western hemisphere could also be the least enjoyable to visit, but the Met is not in New York for nothing. Despite its size (tens of thousands of works of art from prehistory to the present) and its complexity (248 galleries in 18 departments), it positively hums with life, always looking for new ways to make the incredible horde of treasures more accessible. The museum's core was built in 1888 by Central Park's architect Calvert Vaux to house a collection of paintings donated by the Union League Club. The central façade and Great Hall were added by Richard Morris Hunt in 1902 and the 5th Avenue wings by McKim, Mead and White in 1906. Further wings were added by Roche, Dinkeloo and Assoc., 1975-87. Walk up the central steps, plunge into the magisterial Great Hall, spend some time at the Information Desk, and then set off on your voyage of discovery.

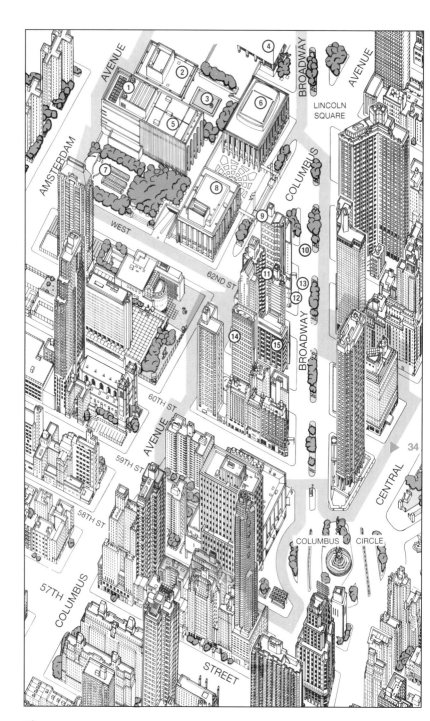

AVENUE

AMSTERDAM

BROADWAY

AVENUE

LINCOLN
SQUARE

COLUMBUS

WEST

62ND ST

BROADWAY

60TH ST

34

59TH ST

AVENUE

58TH ST

CENTRAL

COLUMBUS CIRCLE

57TH

COLUMBUS

STREET

32

Lincoln Center

(1) Built amid controversy in the '60s, the **Lincoln Center for the Performing Arts** succeeds in bringing together the finest music, theater, opera and ballet in New York. The design – classical travertine buildings, grouped around a pedestrian plaza – was based on the Capitoline Hill in Rome. Best vantage point to view the plaza, buzzing with anticipation before curtain-up, is the Met.'s ritzy **Grand Tier** restaurant (**$$$**). (2) **Vivian Beaumont Theater**, a now successful repertory with a chequered past, including three years dark. Downstairs is the experimental **Mitzi E. Newhouse Theater** and upstairs, the **Library and Museum of the Performing Arts**, where exhibits range from costumes and set designs to scripts and scores. (3) **Julliard School of Music and Recital Hall**. A bridge connects the youngest component, and most brutal architecturally, to the rest of the complex. In fact this prestigious school was founded in 1905. (4) **Alice Tully Hall**, designed for recitals and chamber music. (5) With its two vast Chagall murals flanking the entrance and dramatic red-carpeted double staircase, the monumental **Metropolitan Opera House** more than fulfils its role as the Plaza's focal point. (6) **Avery Fisher Hall** has a dashing, pale wood-paneled auditorium, notorious for its indifferent acoustics, which, in addition to concerts, hosts the New York Film Festival. (7) **Guggenheim Band Shell** in **Damrosch Park** stages free outdoor concerts. (8) **New York State Theater**, impressive home of the New York City Ballet and Opera companies. Above the spacious entrance is a magnificent galleried foyer, each of the four levels sporting elaborate gold balcony railings. (9) **O'Neal's** (48 W 63rd St; obscured), lively pub, convenient for a pre-theater snack (**$$**). (10) The revamped **Empire Hotel** (**$$**) provides class, comfort and value for money. (11) The satisfying curves of the **Lincoln Plaza Tower** (1979) hark back to the '30s. Evidence that some culture has spilled over from the Lincoln Center into its environs, (12) **Schirmer Music** store and (13) **The Ballet Shop**, for the accoutrements of the art New Yorkers take most seriously. (14) An Art Deco gem in the wasteland south of the Center, **43 West 61st Street** is a brick high-rise, stylishly embellished, and originally built as one of the first 'automatic' garages (i.e. with a lift). (15) In a '60s mid-rise, with a huge ladder of exposed concrete joists abutting Broadway, the **American Bible Society** displays such rarieties as Dead Sea Scroll fragments and pages of the Gutenberg Bible.

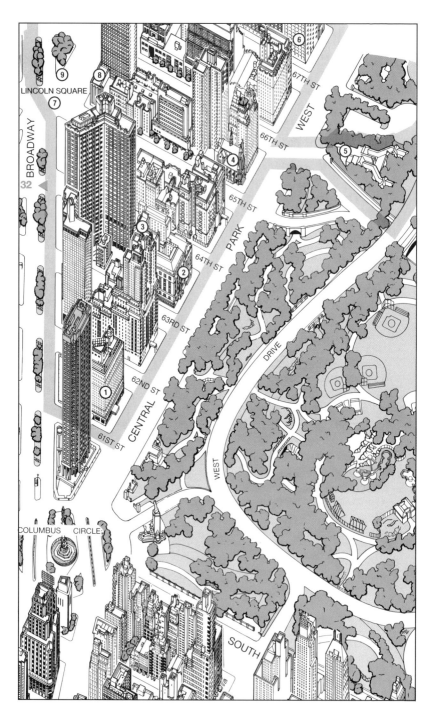

LINCOLN SQUARE

BROADWAY

32

67TH ST

WEST

66TH ST

65TH ST

64TH ST

63RD ST

62ND ST

61ST ST

CENTRAL

PARK

DRIVE

WEST

COLUMBUS   CIRCLE

SOUTH

Central Park West

Central Park West kicks off with a reliable, well-priced hotel, ① the **May-flower ($$)**. ② The **New York Society** for **Ethical Culture** was a welcome dip into Art Nouveau by Robert Kohn in 1910. Behind is ③ the **Westside YMCA** (5 W 63rd St). ④ A pause in the line of fashionable apartment blocks for an attractive church, the **Holy Trinity Lutheran** where church music is performed. ⑤ Food and service may be unpredictable, but New Yorkers will tell you that there is nothing more magical than the **Tavern on the Green's** Crystal Room when snow is falling in Central Park, or its garden on a summer's evening. Trees twinkling with thousands of fairy lights, ponies and traps waiting outside and an unparalleled setting add to the romantic appeal of this famous, if flawed restaurant (**$$$**). ⑥ More romance at the **Café des Artistes** with its nostalgic air enhanced by 1930s murals of chastely disrobed females; animated atmosphere, fine food (**$$$**). Its home is one of West Side's several historic apartment buildings, **Hôtel des Artistes** (1913), where eye-catching architecure attracted a long line of famous residents. Others (all off map) include the **Dakota**, where John Lennon lived and died, **Ansonia** and **Apthorp Apartments**. ⑦ Among a plethora of Lincoln Center eateries **Ginger Man** (51 W 64th St; **$$**) and **Sfuzzi** (58 W 65th St; **$$**; obscured) are noteworthy. The former is marked out by a 50ft-high mock Statue of Liberty on its roof. ⑧ Scheduled to move to W 53rd Street (*see page 44*), this is the temporary home of the **Museum of American Folk Art**, a soothing, pleasing and amusing collection of the best folk art from colonial times to the present. From ⑨ **Lincoln Square, Columbus Avenue** (off map) plunges northwards, strung with pavement cafés, restaurants of all descriptions, all-night food stores and a variety of stores. It is relaxed, alive and always thronged with people. To the west, Amsterdam Avenue, Broadway and West End Avenue track a parallel course through a sea of fine apartment buildings, once neglected, now gentrified. West Side has become the place to live for many monied New Yorkers who find East Side too genteel, too impeccable and unbending for their taste. The two sides of the Park are as different as chalk and cheese, but both are now right, at least up to the mid-80s streets. Don't miss **Zabar's**, an amazing and volatile food emporium and a New York institution (2245 Broadway at 80th St). The **American Museum of Natural History** is on CPW at 79th St (off map).

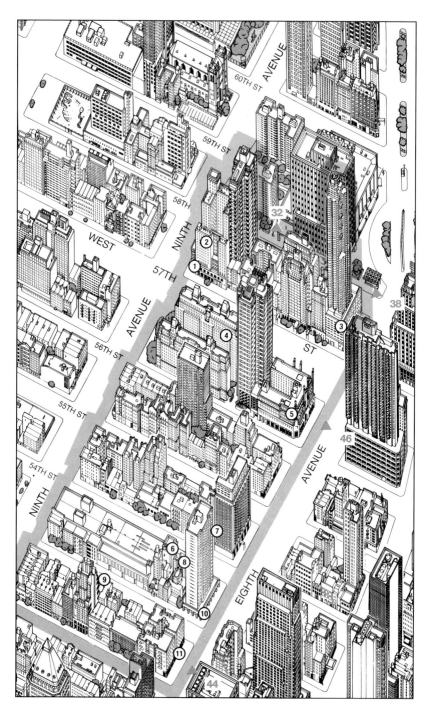

San Juan Hill

Walking south-west from Columbus Circle, the neighborhood deteriorates sharply; streets with the occasional well-to-do apartment building turn into a desolate no-man's-land, bordering Clinton, better known as Hell's Kitchen, the Garment Center and Theater District. ① Centered around the junction of West 57th Street and 9th Avenue, **San Juan Hill** was a black settlement at the turn of the century, which derived its name from the courageous acts of a black unit during the Spanish-American War. ② 353 W 57th Street was built in 1929 as home to the **American Women's Association**. Requisitioned as officers' barracks during the Second World War, it later became the Henry Hudson Hotel and now houses the television company, WNET. If you have a head for heights, a roof-top bridge connects gardens on top of the building's two sections. ③ **One Central Park Place**, slim, sleek high-rise apartment building (1988; Davis and Brody). ④ Henry Mandel's luxury 1930s **Parc Vendôme Apartments**, built on a site intended for a second Metropolitan Opera House that never materialized. ⑤ **Hearst Magazine Building** (1928), an eccentricity built in the style of the Austrian Secession as the base of a high-rise, which explains its sawn-off appearance and the outlandish way the obelisks protrude above roof level. ⑥ **American Theater of Actors** (314 W 54th St; obscured) occupies a 19thC Beaux Arts courthouse, jazzed up with bright colored paintwork. ⑦ Romanesque-style brick building, which began life as offices and is now **St George Tropoforos Hellenic Orthodox Church**. ⑧ Just like *Cagney and Lacey*, it's all action at the NYC Police Department's **Midtown North Precinct**, housed in this pleasing 1930s limestone building, the doorways guarded by attractive Art Deco lamps. ⑨ A jewel in this bleak area, pretty Italianate **St Benedict's Church** (RC). Two other pleasant surprises are the Italian restaurants ⑩ **Da Tommaso** (**$$**), a simple, friendly place, serving hearty regional fare and, slightly more sophisticated, with a sky mural on the ceiling, ⑪ **Caffè Cielo** (**$$**), which attracts theatergoers with its Northern specialities. Both offer value for money.

COLUMBUS CIRCLE

BROADWAY

BROADWAY

WEST

WEST

CENTRAL

57TH

AVENUE

SEVENTH

56TH

55TH

SIXTH AVENUE

STREET

36

46

48

50

1
2
3
4
5
6
7
8
9
10
11
12
13
14

Columbus Circle

Walking north along one of the great Avenues (here Seventh) the vista is no longer blocked by huge buildings as you approach Central Park. A welcome sense of freedom creeps in at the sight of lush greenery and the promise of open spaces. ① **Columbus Circle**, where Broadway brushes the corner of the Park before striking across the Upper West Side, is a grand landmark reduced to an anonymous traffic circle by roaring cars; neither **Columbus** himself (Gaetano Russo, 1892) in the center, nor ② the **Maine Memorial** (Magonigle and Piccirilli, 1913) manage to redeem the situation. ③ The **New York Convention and Visitors Bureau**, housed in a singular Moorish-style building. ④ **Hard Rock Café** (221 W 57th St; obscured). The back end of a Cadillac acting as a canopy marks the spot, famous for its queues, noise, hype and good hamburgers (**$$**). ⑤ *Fin de siècle* elegance for the **Art Students League**. ⑥ Pop into the grim-looking **Osborne's** opulent marble lobby, designed by Tiffany, for a taste of apartment house luxury circa 1885, unchanged since then. Leonard Bernstein wrote the score for *West Side Story* while living here. ⑦ The 1909 façade of **Alwyn Court** (180 W 58th St; obscured) must be seen to be believed; it is positively crawling with dragons. Next door, the world's most expensive food, caviar, is served in suitably exclusive surroundings at **Petrossian** (**$$$**). ⑧ **Hotel Salisbury**: family-size rooms with kitchenettes offer value for money (**$$**). ⑨ Lips and noses seem to have obsessed designer Milton Glaser at the animated **Trattoria Dell' Arte**, which boasts a huge antipasto selection (**$$**). ⑩ **Carnegie Hall** opened in 1891 with a concert conducted by Tchaikovsky and has remained a legendary venue for serious musicians, both classical and popular. It was superbly restored in 1986, having narrowly escaped demolition. ⑪ One of New York's truly idiosyncratic restaurants, the **Russian Tea Room** (150 W 57th St; obscured) is beloved by celebrities for its blinis with caviar, iced vodkas, and wonderfully festive decor (**$$$**). ⑫ There is a nice creepy feeling in the **Mysterious Bookshop**, enhanced by the creaking floorboards, steep spiral staircase, and shelves and shelves of suspense and detective books, both rare and new. ⑬ The French-owned **Parker Meridien** hotel caters for today's body-conscious businessman; there's even a roof-top jogging track (**$$$**). ⑭ **New York Deli** (104 W 57th St; obscured; **$**): an ex-Automat (*see page 103*), '30s décor intact.

AVENUE

67TH ST

66TH ST

65TH ST

FIFTH

64TH ST

AVENUE

63RD ST

MADISON

62ND ST

AVENUE

61ST ST

PARK

60TH ST

50

52

54

40

East Side

When in 1896 the celebrated Mrs Astor escaped the midtown bustle to this airy suburb, society moved with her, and the next years saw a building boom of ornate Renaissance mansions. Many were demolished for luxury apartments, but many still stand; no longer privately owned, but homes to Consuls and Clubs. ① Bastion of the arts, **Lotos Club** occupies this extravagant Beaux Arts mansion, built for Margaret Vanderbilt Shepard. ② Llamas, Muscovy ducks, a painted Noah's ark and toy castle make the **Children's Zoo** a toddlers' paradise. ③ On the site of Mrs Astor's mansion, the imposing Moorish Romanesque **Temple Emanu-El** (1929). ④ Revamped in 1988, the **Zoo** boasts over 100 species, all in near-natural habitats. ⑤ Ivy-clad and castellated, the Department of Parks HQ, built as an **Arsenal** in 1848. ⑥ **Churchills'** window, cluttered with the weird and wonderful from flaking plaster figures to sunglasses with ocean liner frames. ⑦ **Kosciuszko Foundation** in an elegant limestone mansion, once owned by Van Alen, who emigrated to Europe rather than face Prohibition. ⑧ At the turn of a key, tiny ballerinas pirouette and carousel horses bob up and down to a tune in **Rita Ford's Music Boxes**, an enticing shop, selling antique and modern boxes of all shapes and sizes. ⑨ Formidable Beaux Arts **India House**. ⑩ **Wildenstein**, gallery in a grand setting. ⑪ Rose brick colonial gem, **Chase Manhattan Bank** (1932). ⑫ **Madison Avenue**, lined with elegant shops that cater to every East Side need; soft leather from **The Coach Store** (No. 710); polo and hunting saddles from **M.J. Knoud Saddlery** (No. 716); English chintzes from **Laura Ashley** (No. 714); crisp cotton from **E. Braun** (No. 717); French crystal from **Lalique** (No. 680). ⑬ **Le Relais**, very chic, very Parisian, down to the sidewalk tables (**$$**). ⑭ **Fifth Avenue Synagogue** (1956). ⑮ **Arcadia**, a suitably Arcadian mural decorates the walls of this elegant little restaurant, where the cuisine surprises and delights (**$$$**). ⑯ A shocking pink Art Deco entrance greets guests at the small charming **Hotel Lowell** (**$$**). ⑰ Stunning late McKim, Mead and White building, all marble, glass, brass and black details, topped by a 1986 conservatory, houses **The Limited**, casual clothes store. ⑱ Founded by a Park Avenue chef, **Hotel Pierre** spells plush European-style luxury (**$$$**). ⑲ **Metropolitan Club**, in a McKim, Mead and White *palazzo*, founded by J.P. Morgan after he was blackballed by the Union League.

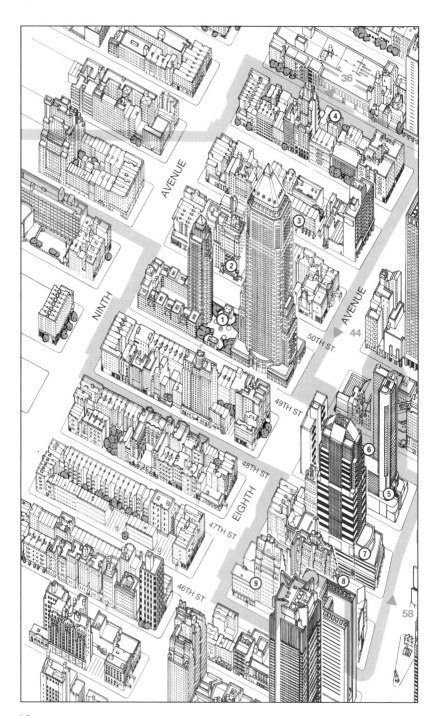

West of Times Square/Clinton

Ninth Avenue marks the western boundary of the Theater District (*see page 57*) and the beginning of the notorious Hell's Kitchen, which has been politely re-named Clinton. This large chunk of central Manhattan, stretching across to the Hudson River and south to the West 30s, was once, like today's Bronx, a fearsome no-go jungle. Here, well into the 20thC, gang warfare held sway and swarms of immigrants toiled in the slaughterhouses and sweatshops, jammed together in the slums. Clinton has improved on those days, but it is still surprisingly resistant to gentrification and remains a fairly desolate area. Here, on the fringes of the Theater District and Clinton, ① **World Wide Plaza** is a bold attempt to move affluent residents and businesses westwards. Constructed in 1989, this giant office/apartment complex stands on the second site of Madison Square Garden (*see page 85*). A clutch of cozy French bistros include ② **Chez Napoleon** (365 W 50th St; **$$**); and ③ **Les Pyrénées**, **Tout Va Bien** (garden in summer) and **Renée Pujol** (Nos 251, 311 and 321 W 51st St, all **$$**). ④ **St Benedict Church**, has a restrained Classical façade (1869). ⑤ The famous old Times Square hotels (Astor, Knickerbocker, and so on) were renowned for their flamboyance and gaiety. Nowadays they are slick and glittery but without personality. This one is the **Crowne Plaza** (**$$$**). ⑥ Theaters here include the **Eugene O'Neill** (230 W 49th St; obscured). The playwright was born, in 1888, in a long-gone hotel on Times Square. Now his theater, which staged Arthur Miller's first big success, *All My Sons* in 1947, is owned by another great American playwright, Neil Simon. ⑦ The **Barrymore** theater remembers another great name, Ethel Barrymore. ⑧ The **Edison** hotel (228 W 47th St; obscured) was designed, in 1931, by one Herbert J. Krapp, who was also responsible for the two theaters mentioned (**$$**). ⑨ **Paramount** hotel (**$$$**), latest adventure in hotel-keeping from the owner/designer team of Ian Schrager and Philippe Starck who brought us the Royalton (*see page 79*). Again a run-down hotel has been transformed into something that has to be seen to be believed. Success is assured: it was booked solidly for a year from its late 1990 opening.

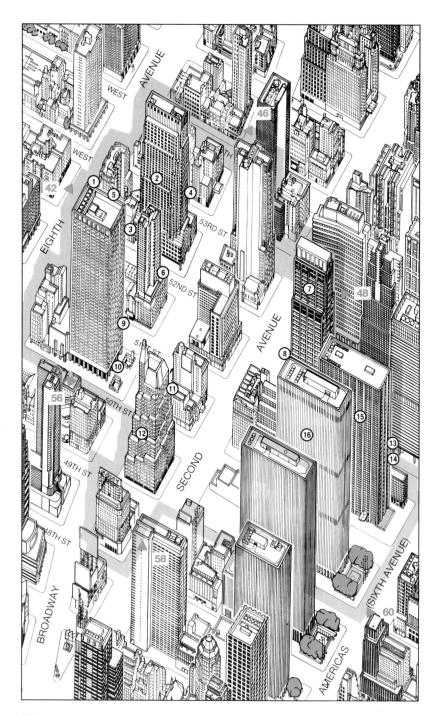

Theater District north

As the city center moved uptown, the Theater District followed. ① Deliciously spicy Thai food, guaranteed to make your tastebuds zing, at **Bangkok Cuisine** (885 8th Ave.; obscured; **$**). ② Green granite high-rise of offices and a theater, **1675 Broadway** was built in 1989 with an architectural debt to the nearby RCA Building (*see page 61*). ③ **Roseland** (239 W 52nd St; obscured), famous dance hall and subject of a movie, where respectable blue-rinsed ladies waltz round a former ice rink with one eye on their steps and the other open for an eligible widower. ④ **Broadway Theater** (1924), host to many famous performances, including Ethel Merman's *Gypsy*. ⑤ **Neil Simon** (250 W 52nd St; obscured), theater which opened as the Alvin in 1927 with the Gershwin musical, *Funny Face*, starring Fred Astaire. ⑥ You can inspect your steak in the window before entering **Gallagher's** (228 W 52nd St; obscured) good old-fashioned steak house, where the steaks are still sizzling when they arrive at the table (**$$$**). ⑦ **Equitable Center** (1986), imposing polished pink granite building, with a handsome atrium, vitalized by a vast Roy Lichtenstein mural. It also contains a branch of the **Whitney Museum of American Art**. ⑧ Devotees of **Bellini by Cipriani** (777 7th Ave.; obscured), sibling of Venetian Harry's Bar, refuse to hear a word said against it, critics claim it is pretentious, and the prices are sky-high. But the pasta is undeniably excellent. 1972 saw two new Broadway theaters, ⑨ the **Gershwin**, and ⑩ **Circle in the Square**, which started life in Greenwich Village and has since achieved both critical acclaim and financial success. Across the road is ⑪ W.A. Swasey's stunning **Winter Garden**, opened by Al Jolson in 1911. Its fame lies in the host of musical hits staged here from *Ziegfeld Follies* to *West Side Story*. ⑫ Stylish office building **750 Seventh Avenue** (1989) by the architects of the Morgan Bank HQ (Roche, Dinkeloo and Associates). ⑬ **Le Bernadin** (155 W 51st St; obscured), impeccable seafood restaurant (**$$$**). ⑭ **Grand Bay Hotel** (152 W 51st St; obscured) combines opulence – crystal chandeliers and marble floors – with the personal touch – bathrobes and bubble bath in every room (**$$$**). Elements of the Rockefeller Center (*see page 61*), ⑮ **Time & Life Building** (1959) and ⑯ **Exxon Building** (1971), both by Harrison, Abramovitz and Harris.

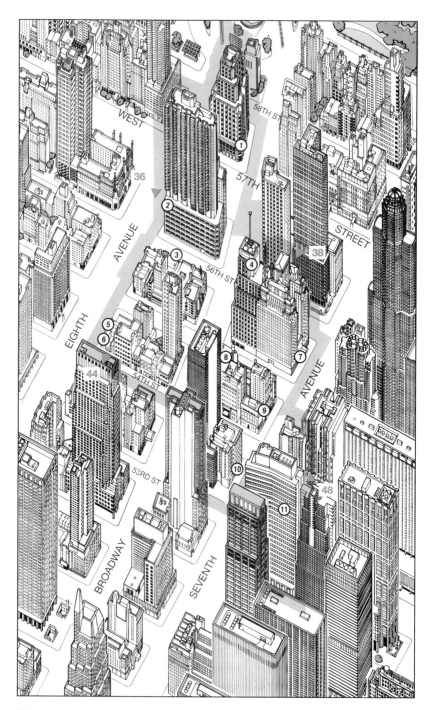

South of Columbus Circle

On the fringe of the Theater District, ① **Coliseum Books** is a friendly bookshop which covers a broad spectrum from sports to computers, best-selling paperbacks to academia, and keeps accommodatingly late hours. ② Outstanding American cuisine in a congenial setting makes **Symphony Café** (950 8th Ave.; obscured) an excellent choice for a light meal before or after a Carnegie Hall concert (**$$**). ③ **India Pavilion** (240 W 56th St; obscured), trusty Indian standby (**$**). ④ **MONY Tower**, 1950s HQ of the Mutual of New York Insurance Company, with a mast that is a high-tech vari-ation on the weathercock. Different colored lights forecast sunshine, cloud, rain and snow; ascending lights indicate an expected rise in temperature; descending ones, a fall. ⑤ Fast but good quality Mexican food and large, lethal Margaritas are to be had at **Caramba**, haunt of a young noisy theater crowd (**$**). Next door at ⑥ **Siam Inn**, exquisite Thai food is on offer in simple no-frills surroundings (**$**). ⑦ The 1980s post-modern lobby and brasserie restaurant of the **Omni Park Central** are a far cry from the '20s and '30s when the hotel was a notorious rendezvous for gangsters and boot-leggers (**$$$**). ⑧ **Broadway Diner** (1726 Broadway; obscured), replica of a '50s diner, where the burgers are not only good but cheap (**$**). ⑨ In the heart of what is affectionately known as 'deliland', the typical kosher **Carne-gie Deli** is probably the most famous in New York, and was captured on cel-luloid in Woody Allen's *Broadway Danny Rose*. Vast helpings guarantee in-digestion, but it is worth it: the pastrami, *blintzes*, corned beef, meat balls and cheesecake are unsurpassed (**$**). ⑩ Pale by comparison, but looking just like something from the set of *Guys and Dolls*, **Stage Deli** (834 7th Ave.) is renowned for its delicious pastrami on rye (**$**). ⑪ **Sheraton Centre**, comfortable, well-run business hotel, with all the personal touches – bathrobes, electric blankets, beds turned down at night – but none of the character and elegance of New York's grandest hotels (**$$$**).

Avenue of the Americas at the mid-Forties

① Art Deco delight, **Hotel Wellington ($$)**. ② Romanesque-style **Ziegfeld Theater** (154 W 55th St; obscured), shows movies now, but started life in the late 1880s as a stable. ③ Ballet and contemporary dance are staged at the **City Center of Music and Drama** (135 W 55th St; obscured), built in 1924 as the **Mecca Temple** – a fact hinted at by its improbable Moorish architecture. ④ Kilner jars of colored jelly beans, licorice and sugar mice will entice anyone with pocket money to spend into the delightfully old-fashioned **Sandler's Sweet Shop** (140 W 55th St; obscured). ⑤ **New York Hilton** (1963), luxury convention hotel with over 2,000 rooms (**$$$**). ⑥ **Corrado**, Northern Italian restaurant with an excellent reputation for pasta and risotto (**$$$**). ⑦ **Hotel Dorset**, comfortable, unpretentious and underrated (**$$$**). ⑧ Nicknamed 'Black Rock', Eero Saarinen's sole skyscraper, the **CBS Building** (1965), is a dignified tower of dark gray granite. ⑨ Caesar Pelli's luxury apartment building, **Museum Tower**, built in 1983 to give financial support to ⑩ the **Museum of Modern Art**, affectionately known as MOMA and housed in a stunning, streamlined and, before additions, pure International Style building (1939). The cream of MOMA's collection includes works by Picasso, Matisse, Hopper, de Kooning and Rothko, Bauhaus textiles and furniture, and departments of film and architecture. Perhaps the *pièce de résistance* is Philip Johnson's tranquil **Sculpture Garden**. ⑪ All kinds of crafts in all kinds of materials – some serious, some jokey – in the **American Craft Museum** (40 W 53rd St; obscured). ⑫ **MOMA Design Store** (44 W 53rd St; obscured), the place to buy a Le Corbusier *chaise longue*, an Eileen Gray table, or an executive desk toy. ⑬ The fluted columns in the **E.F. Hutton Building** (Roche, Dinkeloo and Associates, 1986) were prototypes for Central Park Zoo (*see page 41*). ⑭ **Donnell Library Center**, branch of the New York Public Library, founded with a legacy from a textile merchant. ⑮ Aluminum-clad **Tishman Building**. ⑯ Bogus Gothic **St Thomas' Church** (1914). ⑰ New premises of the excellent **Museum of TV and Radio**. ⑱ **21 Club**, figures of famous jockeys ride the railings outside this former speakeasy, today a rallying point for high society.

Fifth Avenue at West 57th Street

Stiff with exclusive apartments, hotels, galleries and shops, Fifth Avenue, just south of the Park, has earned the nickname 'The Gold Coast'. ① Modeled on the London Ritz, the **Ritz-Carlton** (**$$$**) is decorated in true British fashion with chintzes and hunting prints; the best rooms enjoy expansive views of the Park. Its restaurant, **The Jockey Club**, with horsey décor to match the name, is popular for power lunches (**$$$**). ② **St Moritz** (50 Central Park South; obscured), business hotel (**$$**), better known for its delightful sidewalk Café de la Paix and ice-cream parlor Rumpelmayer's, which serves unforgettable hot chocolate and sells soft toys. ③ Morning-fresh fish, superb desserts and an outstanding wine list put **Manhattan Ocean Club** (57 W 58th St; obscured) in the running for best seafood restaurant (**$$$**). ④ **Wyndham Hotel** (42 W 58th St; obscured), excellent value, yet classy enough to appeal to actors doing stints on Broadway (**$$**). ⑤ Controversial variation in skyscraper architecture, the sloping **Solow Building**, sister of the Grace Building (*see page 79*). ⑥ Manhattan landmark in its own right, Hardenbergh's majestic turn-of-the-century **Plaza Hotel** (**$$$**). Its thick-carpeted, gilded opulence has always attracted the rich and famous, from Frank Lloyd Wright to the Beatles. Take tea in the splendid **Palm Court**, cocktails in the **Oak Bar**, full of dark wood and chat, dinner at **Trader Vic's** (**$$**) or the excellent **Oyster Bar** (**$$$**). ⑦ Behind an attractive 1905 cast-iron façade, **Rizzoli Bookstore** is charming and oak-paneled. Browse through its distinguished art section to the strains of Bach or Mozart. ⑧ Hushed shrine to fashion, **Bergdorf Goodman** oozes style from its marble floors to the racks of stunning clothes by Armani, Lacroix, Ralph Lauren and the like. ⑨ **West 57th Street**, home to a host of art galleries. ⑩ **Charivari 57** (18 W 57th St; obscured), cutting-edge clothes for men and women. ⑪ In 1929 MOMA's first gallery (*see page 49*) opened in Warren and Wetmore's **Crown Building**; today it houses **Bulgari** and **Ferragamo**. ⑫ **Darbar** (44 W 56th St; obscured), a corner of India with authentic dcor and mouth-watering Mogul dishes (**$$**). ⑬ **OMO Norma Kamali** (11 W 57th St; obscured), innovative fashion from leopard-skin bikinis to satin wedding dresses. ⑭ 'King of Diamonds' **Harry Winston** sells superior stones in flamboyant settings. ⑮ In keeping with its precepts, **Fifth Avenue Presbyterian Church** has a somber air, both in its neo-Gothic façade and dark wood-fitted bowl interior.

The Plaza

Nowhere in New York is the magnetism and power of the place more immediately felt than along Fifth Avenue as it draws near to Central Park. After ① **The Plaza**, the Avenue's magnificent shops and hotels give way to equally great residences which border Central Park. ② The equestrian statue of **General Sherman** (1900) is so gold it looks like a trinket from a souvenir stall. Much more gracious is ③ Carrère and Hastings' **Pullitzer Fountain** (1915). Horse-drawn carriages can be hired from the Plaza for romantic rides in Central Park. ④ The **General Motors Building** (1963), breaks up the intimate grandeur of The Plaza with its soaring stripes of white Georgia marble and black glass. In front is a sunken mini-plaza, complete with fake grass carpet. The GM Building is the new home of ⑤ **F.A.O. Schwarz** (obscured), legendary toy shop stuffed with life-size giraffes, scaled-down sports cars and the like. On the opposite (SE) corner of E 58th Street is the spectacular new **Bergdorf Goodman Mens Store**. ⑥ **57th Street** is New York's smartest shopping street, with a classy mix of clothes and beauty stores, jewelers and art galleries. This stretch includes **Laura Ashley** (No. 21), **Jaeger** (No. 19), **Wally Findlay Gallery** (No. 17), **Hermès** (No. 11), **Burberry's** (No. 9), **Chanel** (No. 5) and **Ann Taylor** (No. 3), specializing in day clothes that appeal to all ages and types. ⑦ Don't be intimidated by **Tiffany's** (727 5th Ave.; obscured). For all its dazzle and glamor, it is an approachable store where you can find something surprisingly reasonable to take home in a sought-after Tiffany gift box. ⑧ **Trump Tower**, a monument to the greed and folly of the l980s. Its six-story atrium of exclusive shops is sheer unbounded ostentation. Along this stretch of 5th Avenue, as far as E 53rd Street, you will find **Steuben Glass** (No. 717), **Godiva Chocolatier** (No. 701), **Elizabeth Arden** (No. 691), **Gucci** (No. 683) and **Fortunoff** (No. 681). ⑨ **La Côte Basque** (5 E 55th St; obscured). Classic French cuisine served with pomp in a picturesque quayside setting (**$$$**). ⑩ The soulless galleria of the **AT&T Building** includes the famous **Quilted Giraffe**, with its one-off cooking and one-off prices (**$$$**). ⑪ In a similar league, and beautifully decorated, is **Prunelle** (18 E 54th St; obscured; $$$). ⑫ Only New Yorkers could refer to tiny **Paley** as a **Park**.

East Side at 57th Street

At the point where Midtown meets the East Side ① **Madison Avenue**'s shops take a step up-market: there's **Cole-Haan** at No. 667 for trendy shoes; at No. 625 **Movado** sells snazzy accessories, from watches to handbags, and **Baccarat** has a fabulous selection of fine crystal and china; **Lederer** (No. 613) has branched out from classic leather goods into clothes for country gents. ② Sensational American/French restaurant, **Aureole** (34 E 61st St; obscured), with multi-talented chef Charles Palmer at the helm (**$$$**). ③ **Grolier Club**, after a 16thC French bibliophile, boasts a marvelous collection of rare books. ④ **Christ Church** (Methodist), a charismatic fake, built in 1932 to appear ancient. ⑤ New York's outpost of the London auctioneer **Christie's** rubs shoulders with showy disco/restaurant **Regine's** (**$$$**). ⑥ Witty curved bands, tiered at the top, give 505 Park Avenue, the old **Aramco Building**, the appearance of a tall ocean liner. ⑦ Graceful Skidmore, Owings and Merrill **Amro Bank Building**, designed for Pepsi-Cola in 1960, and its equally elegant 1986 neighbor, **500 Park Avenue Tower**. ⑧ Monochrome Art Deco treat, the **Fuller Building**, home to a throng of exclusive galleries. ⑨ Where bookstalls once lined the sidewalk, wood-paneled **Argosy** (116 E 59th St; obscured) sells antiquarian books, prints and maps. ⑩ **T. Anthony**, the shop where the jet-set buys its luggage. ⑪ Brand new **Regent of New York**, where rooms have computers and faxes for executives who only pause to take a sunken bath (**$$$**). ⑫ Distinctive 42-story stepped **Ritz Tower** apartment hotel. ⑬ **Banana Republic** for fun casual clothes at affordable prices. ⑭ Super smart shoes for the super rich at **Helene Arpels**. ⑮ Supreme Japanese cuisine in tranquil surroundings at **Mitsukoshi** (**$$$**). ⑯ Galleries specializing in everything from Persian rugs to medical instruments cover 50,000 square feet in **Place des Antiquaires**. ⑰ Along **East 57th Street**, a miscellany of glossy shops are devoted to designer fashion (**Guy Laroche** No. 36); exotic shoes (**Maud Frizon** No. 49); status-symbol luggage (**Louis Vuitton** No. 51); hand-made silver (**Buccellati** No. 46); up-market hardware, knobs and knockers at **William Hunrach** (No. 153); and high-tech gadgets at **Hammacher Schlemmer** (No. 147).

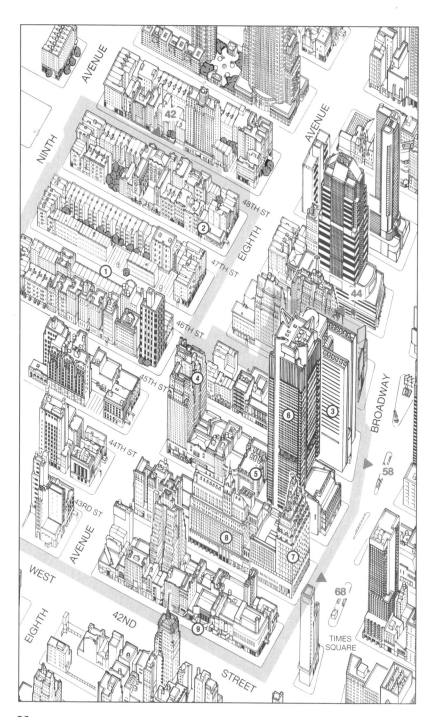

Theater District

The heart of New York's Theater District is Times Square (*see page 69*). The streets are crammed with theaters too numerous to mention, each one the scene of some actor's triumph, another playwright's undoing. This is 'Broadway'. ① Theatergoers need feeding and West 46th St is known as 'restaurant row'. *Grande dame* is the Italian **Barbetta** (No. 321; **$$$**), famed for her beautiful garden but now very elderly. Others include: actors' favorites and brother establishments **Orso**, chic Italian (No. 322; **$$**) and **Joe Allen**, brick walls, simple food (No. 326; **$$**); **Le Rivage**, bistro (No. 340; **$$**); **Audrone**, French (No. 342; **$$**); **Carolina**, southern cooking (No. 355; **$$**) and **Lattanzi**, Jewish-Roman (No. 361; **$$**). Over in West 47th St are ② **Trixie's** carnival restaurant, best with a crowd (**$$**), and next door upbeat **B. Smith's** (**$$**). ③ **Marriot Marquis** hotel (**$$$**), a frivolous piece of architecture which cost the demolition of three theaters. Glass elevators whizz through the world's tallest atrium to a revolving restaurant at the top, aptly named **The View** (**$$$**). ④ **Milford Plaza** hotel, dull, modernized, inexpensive (**$$**). Amongst a clutch of theaters on this block are ⑤ the **Shubert** and **Booth** (both 1913) with ornate interiors. They back onto **Shubert Alley** where aspiring actors hung round the eponymous impresario's offices hoping to be spotted. ⑥ **One Astor Plaza** (1969), topped by a peculiar set of fins, replaced the famous Astor Hotel whose florid façade encapsulated the now long-vanished 'gay nineties' mood of Times Square. Thankfully ⑦ the terrific **Paramount Building** (Rapp and Rapp, 1926) is still intact. Look up. ⑧ The offices of the **New York Times**. Journalists have direct access to **Sardi's** (234 W 44th St; obscured), once the playground of every star in town – now they've all moved on (**$$$**). ⑨ This stretch of 42nd Street is known as 'sin street', although grim street would be more appropriate. Amongst the movie houses the boarded-up **New Amsterdam** (214 W 42nd St; obscured) stands out as a typical tale of woe. With a superb Art Nouveau interior it was the celebrated home of the Ziegfeld Follies from 1913 till 1927. In the '70s it became a Kung Fu movie house and in the '80s it closed.

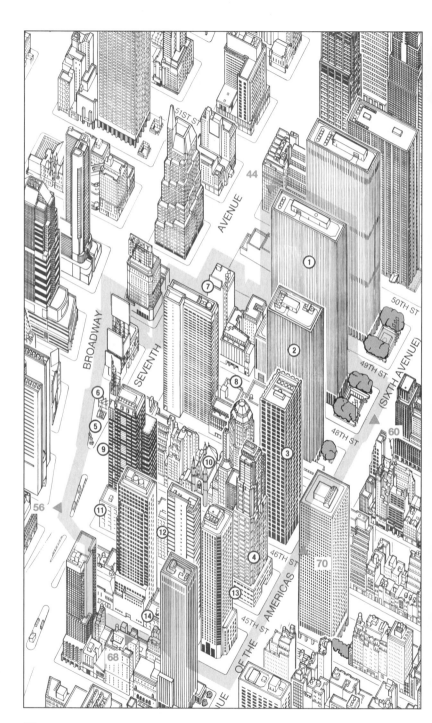

Times Square North

The splendid Rockefeller Center has spawned a stream of unmemorable, box-like skyscrapers which line the Avenue of the Americas (Sixth Avenue) like sentries. Shown here, for identification, are ① the **McGraw-Hill Building**, ② the **Celanese Building**, ③ the **J.P. Stevens Tower**, and ④ the brand new **Americas Tower**. ⑤ Would First World War hero Father Francis Duffy, and songwriter George Cohen be surprised to know that they have ended up co-habiting **Duffy Square**, scruffy island at the northern end of Times Square? Their statues serve a useful purpose, being something to look at when queuing for half-price, same-day theater tickets at ⑥ the **TKTS** booth. ⑦ A good bookshop, specializing in all aspects of the theater, is **Drama Bookshop** (723 7th Ave.; obscured). ⑧ Two terrific musical instrument stores in 48th Street are **Manny's** (No. 156) and **Sam Ash** (Nos 155, 160 and 166) both founded in the 1920s. Manny's walls are plastered with autographed photos of the store's many famous customers. ⑨ Spot the famous ladies. Marilyn Miller, Mary Pickford, Ethel Barrymore and Rosa Ponselle are sculpted on to the front of the former **I. Miller** shoestore. The perpetrator, in 1929, was A. Stirling Calder, father of Alexander. ⑩ **Church of St Mary-the-Virgin** (RC; 1895). ⑪ The most pleasing of Times Square's new hotels, the **Eichner ($$$)**. ⑫ The neo-Baroque **Lyceum Theater** (obscured), with its wavy canopy and powerful columns, is the oldest New York theater still in operation for legitimate productions. Built in 1903 by masters of the art, Herts and Tallant. ⑬ Like all good ethnic restaurants, the strength of **Cabana Carioca** (123 W 45th St; obscured) lies in the food, so brave the steep staircase and gaudy décor and press on. You will be rewarded with cheap heaps of tasty Brazilian fare – black bean stew (*feijoada*), sucking pig, shrimp *paulista, caldo verde* (**$$**). ⑭ **Café Un Deux Trois** (123 W 44th St; obscured) is one European ex-pat's very favorite New York restaurant. It has the feel of a relaxed yet sophisticated Paris bistro, with typically straightforward bistro food, plus the added attraction of paper tablecloths and a set of crayons for doodling. The building (1894) is handsome.

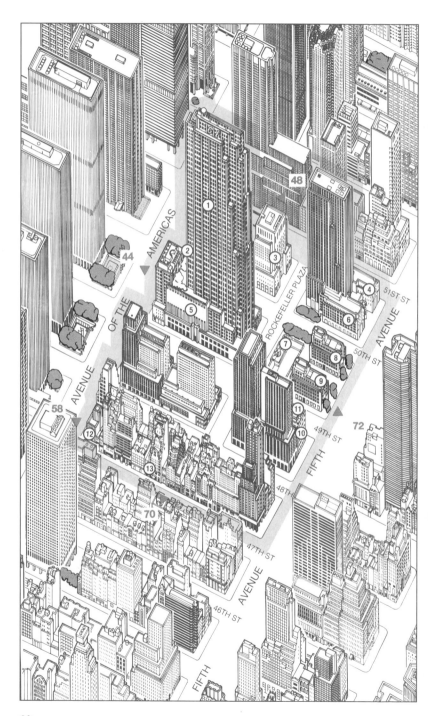

AMERICAS

OF THE

AVENUE

44

58

ROCKEFELLER PLAZA

48

AVENUE

51ST ST

50TH ST

FIFTH

49TH ST

72

48TH

47TH ST

46TH ST

70

AVENUE

FIFTH

① ② ③ ④ ⑤ ⑥ ⑦ ⑧ ⑨ ⑩ ⑪ ⑫ ⑬

60

Rockefeller Center

John D. Rockefeller Jr's ambitious 'city within a city' comprises a complex of offices, shops, theaters and open spaces, covering 22 acres. He acquired the land to provide a new home for the Metropolitan Opera, but the Depression scuppered the Met.'s plans, and John D. was left in the '30s to develop the site himself. ① Dominating the rest, the 70-story tiered **RCA (now GE) Building** is elegant in its simplicity. Although not one of Manhattan's tallest skyscrapers, there is a terrific view from the 65th-floor **Rainbow Room Restaurant ($$$)**. With its fabulous revolving dance floor and meticulous Art Deco details, it's like stepping onto the set of *Top Hat*. The building's 1250 Avenue of the Americas entrance is strikingly decorated with mosaic tiles, depicting a host of symbolic figures. ② All the big showbiz names from Charlie Chaplin to Frank Sinatra have played **Radio City Music Hall** (1932; obscured), the world's largest theater. ③ In **Associated Press Building**, the **New York Bound Bookshop** is a must for all visitors. Floor-to-ceiling shelves are crammed with every available guide to the city. The friendly owners will steer you in the right direction and provide a comfy chair in which to browse. ④ Already in Hitler's grasp in 1935, Germany never procured its Deutsche Haus as intended and this building became **International House** instead; one of four buildings devoted to different countries, with massive bronze doorways, each decorated with appropriate motifs. ⑤ For the uninitiated, there is a fascinating tour of the **NBC Studios**. ⑥ **Palazzo d'Italia** (1935). ⑦ In **Rockefeller Plaza**, pedestrian heart of the complex, a statue of Prometheus keeps a golden eye on skaters on the outside rink from October till early May, when the ice is melted and restaurant tables occupy the space, among them those of the excellent **Sea Grill ($$$)**. The Plaza's classy shops include **Crabtree and Evelyn**, **Jaeger** and **Teuscher Chocolatier**. The flower-filled promenade between ⑧ **British Empire Building** and ⑨ **La Maison Française** is aptly called **Channel Gardens**. ⑩ An ornate Art Deco lobby is tucked away in the **Goelet Building**. ⑪ Chic French restaurant, **La Resèrve** (4 W 49th St, obscured); **($$$)**. ⑫ **Kaplan's**, scruffy but authentic Diamond District deli. ⑬ **Gotham Book Mart & Gallery**, bursting at the seams with books, and known for its strong section on 20thC literature.

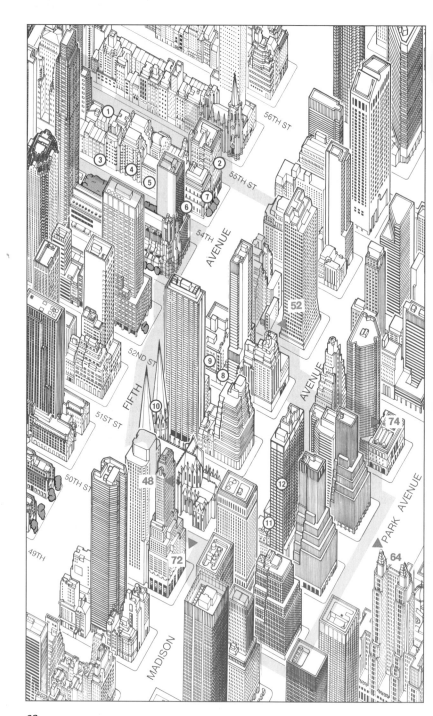

56TH ST

55TH ST

54TH AVENUE

52ND ST

FIFTH

51ST ST

50TH ST

49TH

MADISON

AVENUE

PARK AVENUE

52

74

48

12

11

72

64

St Patrick's Cathedral

Along the stretch of Fifth Avenue that was once the domain of Astors and Vanderbilts, magnificent mansions still stand, now occupied by exclusive shops, hotels and restaurants. ① Hot butter croissants, brioches and baguettes – all freshly baked – from **J.P. French Bakery** (54 W 55th St; obscured). ② Ornate Belle Epoque details were superimposed on the **Peninsula Hotel ($$$)** during a previous incarnation as Maxim's de Paris. Before that it was the Gotham, haunt of movie stars. As well as sumptuous marble bathrooms, it boasts an elegant French restaurant, **Adrienne ($$$)**. ③ In a pretty brownstone, **Restaurant Raphael ($$$)** serves some of the best nouvelle cuisine in town. ④ **Rockefeller Apartments**, built in 1936 by John D. Jr. Two distinctive columns with wrap-around windows guard both ends, enjoying a view of the MOMA garden (*see page 49*). ⑤ The lower floors of the house Nelson Rockefeller used as a private office are now occupied by **Aquavit ($$$)**, a Scandinavian restaurant that is like a breath of fresh air; its soaring atrium, filled with birch trees, has a waterfall at one end. The food is equally stunning. Two fanciful McKim, Mead and White creations ⑥ **Petrola House** (Nos 9-11; obscured), and ⑦ the even more outlandish **University Club**. ⑧ Classic French restaurant **La Grenouille ($$$)**, reputed to spend $100,000 a year on flowers alone. ⑨ The splendid Italianate mansion that now makes a fitting home for **Cartier** (2 E 52nd St; obscured) was allegedly given to the family in 1917 by the owner's wife, Mrs Morton F. Plant, in exchange for a string of pearls. ⑩ Mock French Gothic, but without the flying buttresses, **St Patrick's Cathedral** was built in 1878-80 by James Renwick Jr. Unlike the great French cathedrals it mimics, it lacks that awe-inspiring quality that makes your spine tingle. ⑪ **Villard Houses** (1884), six separate mansions designed to look like a single Italian Renaissance palace, commissioned by publisher Henry Villard and built by . . . guess who? McKim, Mead and White. It contains two interesting book-shops: **Sky Books**, a mail order company that mushroomed into the world's largest selection on military history, and architecturally-biassed **Urban Center Books**. In 1980 the new owner Harry Helmsley spared the building from demolition and incorporated two of the mansions into ⑫ his luxury **Helmsley Palace Hotel ($$$)**, which in stark contrast is an immense glass tower. Spectacular in its opulence, the hotel is presided over by the indomitable Leona Helmsley.

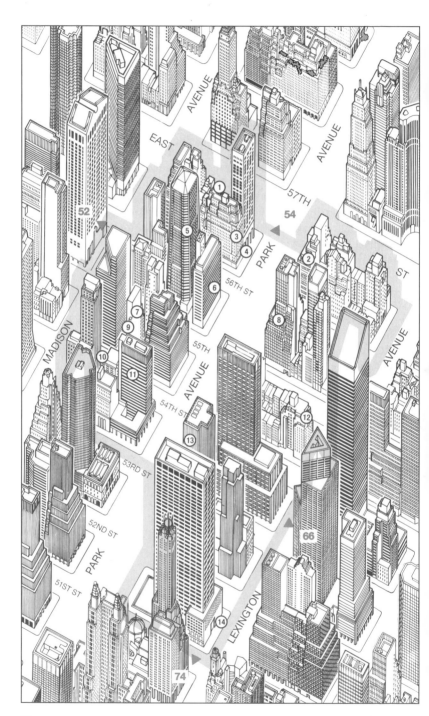

EAST

AVENUE

AVENUE

57TH

54

52

PARK

ST

① ①
③
④
⑤
56TH ST
② ②
⑥
⑦
AVENUE
⑨
MADISON
⑧
⑩
55TH
⑪
54TH ST
⑫
AVENUE
⑬
53RD ST
52ND ST
66
PARK
LEXINGTON
⑭
51ST ST
74

64

In an area of architectural and real wealth, evident in the abundance of exclusive shops, restaurants and hotels, ① **Pace Gallery** (32-34 E 57th St; obscured) shows celebrated American artists and other important collections. ② Beneath the stylish fashion boutique, **Matsuda** (461 Park Ave.; obscured), is an equally stylish Japanese restaurant, **Mitsukoshi**, where you can savor exquisite sushi at a price (**$$$**). ③ **Swissôtel Drake** (1927), famous in the '60s as home to New York's first disco, Shepheards. Now Swiss-owned and fastidiously run, it boasts one of the city's finest restaurants, **Lafayette**. A startlingly creative menu embraces Swiss and French cuisine, from which skillfully prepared dishes rarely disappoint (**$$$**). ④ **Susan Bennis/Warren Edwards**, for dramatic shoes in colorful suede, silk or baby croc, but sit down when they tell you how much. ⑤ Smart stripes distinguish glossy **Park Avenue Tower**. ⑥ **Mercedes-Benz showroom** (1955), Frank Lloyd Wright's first excursion in New York. ⑦ Empire State lookalike, **Heron Tower** (1987). ⑧ **Universal Pictures Building** (1947), the first office building in a residential stretch of Park Avenue, and the first to conform to the 'wedding cake' design stipulated by the zoning laws. ⑨ **Le Cygne** (55 E 54th St; obscured) provides an elegant post-modern setting in which to sample classic French food (**$$$**). ⑩ **Elysée Hotel** (60 E 54th St; obscured), with its old-fashioned charm, probably still feels much as it did when Tallulah Bankhead checked in (**$$$**). Its restaurant, **Pisces**, serves excellent seafood (**$$**). ⑪ **Lever House** (Skidmore, Owings and Merrill, 1952) furnished Park Avenue with its first glass wall. ⑫ Henry Fernbach's Moorish Revival **Central Synagogue** (1872) is the city's oldest permanent synagogue. Its brownstone façade is enlivened by bronze cupolas, but outshined by the exuberant stenciled interior. ⑬ Mies van der Rohe's quintessentially Modernist bronze and glass **Seagram Building** (1958), with interior by Philip Johnson, was the realization of his vision for Berlin in the '20s. A meal at its restaurant **The Four Seasons** is an experience, from the sight of Picasso's backdrop in the lobby to the tantalizing menu; a haunt of media tycoons (**$$$**). **The Brasserie** is open 24 hours a day for light meals (**$$**). ⑭ The very **subway vent** which emitted the gust that lifted Marilyn Monroe's skirt in the famous scene from *The Seven Year Itch*.

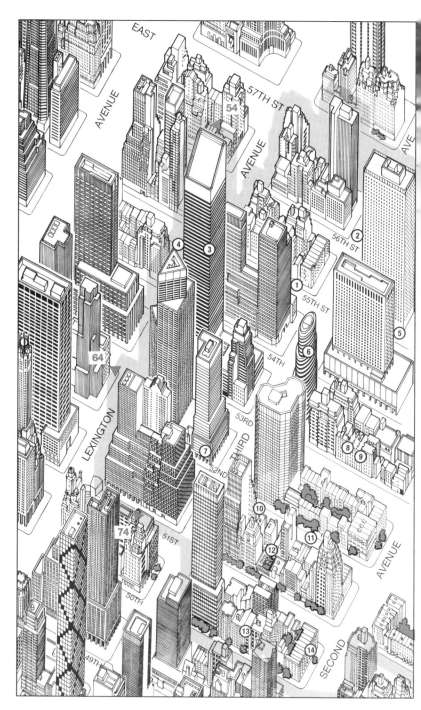

Citicorp Center

In a neighborhood teeming with restaurants, ① **Shun Lee Palace** (155 E 55th St; obscured) is the original member of the chain that introduced up-market Chinese food to New York (**$$**). ② **P.J. Clarke's** (915 3rd Ave.; obscured) started life as an old-fashioned Irish saloon and has ended up as a singles' bar, where yuppies jostle for cocktails and burgers. ③ Hugh Stubbins' **Citicorp Center** (1978), a post-modern aluminum skyscraper, perched on ten-story-high anti-earthquake stilts, with a ski-jump roof. Inside, the atrium – scene of pop concerts – is devoted to a **market** of shops and restaurants. Nestling in its shadow is ④ the 1970s granite **St Peter's Lutheran Church** (obscured), known for its jazz at Evensong and innovative crypt theater. ⑤ There is also jazz Mon-Sat at **Michael's Pub** (211 E 55th St; obscured), where Woody Allen rarely misses his Mon night stint on the clarinet (**$$**). ⑥ In Philip Johnson's aptly named **Lipstick Building** (1986), you can sample Tuscan cuisine, less robust than is traditional, at the starkly trendy **Toscana ($$$)**, or grab an antipasto and espresso at **Gran Caffè Bitici ($$)**. ⑦ Elegant Japanese restaurant, **Nippon** has an excellent reputation, particularly for its authentic *kaiseki* (**$$**). ⑧ **Tiny Doll House**, minute shop selling everything you need to kit out a dollhouse from miniature beds, chests, kettles, knives and forks to the tiny inhabitants themselves. ⑨ Renowned for *porcini* and other Northern Italian specialties, **Il Nido** attracts a sophisticated East Side clientele and leaves a large dent in their wallets (**$$$**). ⑩ The shop professional cooks use for their equipment, **Bridge Kitchenware** (214 E 52nd St; obscured) is crammed with every utensil and gadget imaginable, plus some striking copper pots and French china. ⑪ Eccentric little hiccough of brick, steel and glass in a traditional terrace, 242 E 52nd Street (obscured) was built in 1950 by Philip Johnson as a **guesthouse for MOMA** (*see page 49*). ⑫ **Greenacre Park**, donated to the city by John D. Rockefeller Jr's daughter. ⑬ Reserve months ahead to ensure a table at New York's most famous French restaurant, 27-year-old **Lutèce**, masterminded by owner-chef André Soltner. Though accused of resting on its laurels in recent years, it still draws the punters in droves to sample the original Alsatian dishes (**$$$**). ⑭ Another owner-chef Zarela Martinez has successfully raised the standing of Mexican food with the original dishes she serves at **Zarela ($$)**.

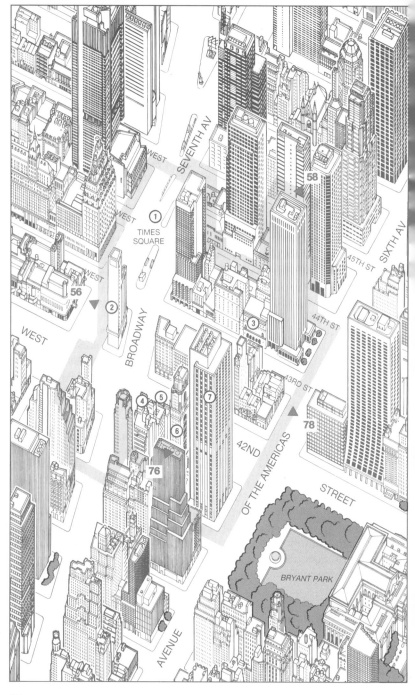

Times Square

(1) **Times Square** is New York's painted face, the one with too much rouge and lipstick and cheap baubles for earrings. It is brash, seedy and vulgar, yet a vibrant focal point of the city, center of the Theater District (*see page 57*). Lavish music halls began opening here in the 1880s and '90s. In the 1920s movies and the famous neon lights electrified the scene. Offices and hotels have pushed in where they can. By the 1970s the inherent sleaziness of the area took a stranglehold that despite several clean-up campaigns (there is one currently in progress involving major rebuilding schemes in the vicinity) won't let go. It is not an area in which to linger after dark. (2) Looking like an upside-down meat cleaver, **One Times Square** was built in 1904 as the headquarters of the *New York Times,* which quickly spread to larger premises across the road. Its arrival prompted Longacre Square to become Times Square, and triggered the famous annual New Year's Eve festivities: the paper celebrated its arrival on December 3lst 1904 with a firework display and the dropping of a lighted sphere (now an apple) down the flagpole at midnight. In 1966 Allied Chemical moved in and gave the terracotta-clad building the slick modern treatment with a new marble skin. They sold in the mid-1970s and now it is just another office block with an uncertain future. (3) McKim, Mead and White's **Town Hall** has a much-praised concert auditorium, intimate and acoustically superb. (4) This building, or at least its shell (142 W 42nd St/1466 Broadway; obscured) was once the glorious **Knickerbocker Hotel**. Enrico Caruso lived here from 1908 until 1920 in a sumptuous apartment; on a few memorable occasions he serenaded the crowd below from his balcony. (5) Out front is **Hotalings** (obscured), specialists in regional and foreign magazines and newspapers since 1905. (6) Tall and pencil-thin – 480ft grown from a plot only 50ft wide – **Bush Tower** (1918). Next door, separated by a watery little plaza, is (7) the **New York Telephone Building** (1974), the first of the boring box towers that march northwards along Avenue of the Americas towards Rockefeller Center (*see page 61*).

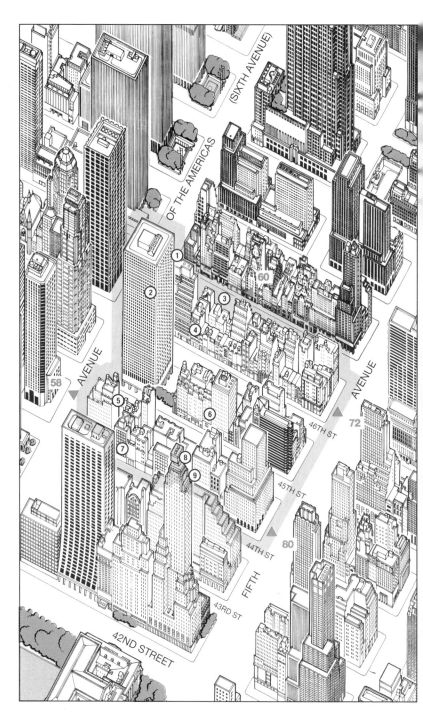

(SIXTH AVENUE)

OF THE AMERICAS

AVENUE

AVENUE

FIFTH

58

60

72

80

46TH ST

45TH ST

44TH ST

43RD ST

42ND STREET

Mid-Forties at Fifth Avenue

① Built in 1962 as the Phoenix Building, Emery Roth's artfully tiered **1180 Avenue of the Americas**. ② **No. 1166 Avenue of the Americas** (1973), a well-designed Skidmore, Owings and Merrill office building with a welcome brick plaza, favored by fresh-air fiends at lunchtime. ③ Bustling **Forty-Seventh Street**, New York's Diamond Center and the province of orthodox Jewish merchants, is lined with tawdry little shops, crammed with flashy gold jewelry and large sparkling gems. ④ **Wentworth**, neither large nor lavish, but this small, reasonably priced hotel affords all the essentials (**$**). ⑤ Take the advice contained in the name of this small, highly-regarded Italian restaurant, **Pasta Prego** (72 W 45th St; obscured), for the pasta is outstanding (**$$**). ⑥ A basement paradise for railway buffs of all ages, **The Train Shop**. ⑦ Goldwin Starett's turn-of-the-century Renaissance-style **Algonquin Hotel**, endearingly down-at-heel and long ago singled out by the literati as a congenial meeting-place. In the 1920s that famous luncheon club, the Round Table, whose members included Dorothy Parker, Robert Benchley and other contributors to *The New Yorker*, used to meet in the **Oak Room** to pit their caustic wits. Today the restaurant has a reputation for outstanding cabaret (**$$**). The cozy paneled **Blue Bar**, its walls lined with Thurber cartoons, is perfect for before or after-dinner drinks. ⑧ Founder of the America's Cup, the **New York Yacht Club** (37 W 44th St; obscured) is housed in a whimsical sculpted Beaux Arts building designed by Warren and Wetmore (1900), with three bay windows, shaped like the sterns of 17thC sailing ships, the ocean spilling over their sills. ⑨ Bastion of the Ivy League, McKim, Mead and White's neo-Georgian **Harvard Club** (1894) boasts an impressive clubby interior, with gilt-framed portraits hanging on red walls and huge shaded chandeliers.

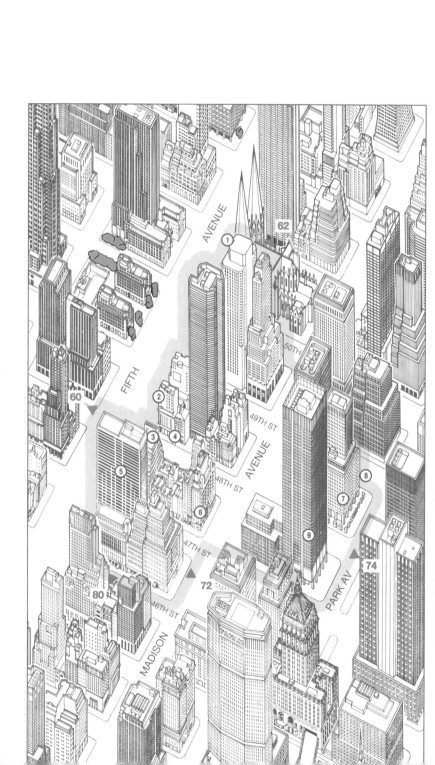

Fifth Avenue at Saks

(1) **Saks Fifth Avenue** (611 5th Ave.; obscured). Dignified and unruffled, this is one department store where you won't get lost and where you will find someone helpful to serve you. Clothes that are fashionable but never gimmicky are its *raison d'être*, with five floors for women and a luxurious men's department. (2) Fifth Avenue's most attractive storefront is its oldest (1913): **Brentano's,** formerly Scribner's, is graced by a two-story, wrought-iron and glass façade which adds great character to the block. Inside, books are displayed in a vast vaulted double-height space. (3) Fondue, courteously presented by waitresses in national dress, is the obvious choice at old-timer **Chalet Suisse** (6 E 48th St; obscured; **$$**). (4) **Hatsuhana**: 'best sushi in town' (**$$**). (5) **575 Fifth Avenue** has a stone skin and, inside, a flashy shopping galleria, a watered-down version of the Trump Tower's. (6) One of Madison Avenue's many venerable shops, **Crouch and Fitzgerald** has been selling luggage and bags since 1839. (7) **Bankers Trust Building**, one neat block atop another. Around the corner is (8) classy restaurant **Aurora** (60 E 49th St; obscured; $$$), designed by Milton Glaser, who had bubbles on the mind at the time – peek in and see. The food may vary in quality, but the leather chairs remain blissfully comfortable. (9) The elevators in **270 Park Avenue** start on the second floor. That's because this black and white steel and gray glass high-rise (Skidmore, Owings and Merrill, 1960) was built over Grand Central Station and there was no room to sink elevator shafts below ground level.

AVENUE

PARK

62

①

②

④

64

53RD ST

52ND

AVENUE

③

⑤

51ST

66

⑦

⑥

72

⑨

50TH

LEXINGTON

82

⑩

49TH ST

⑧

AV

⑪

⑫

48TH ST

THIRD

47TH ST

94

Park Avenue at 50th Street

① Stately **Park Avenue**, with its banks of flowers and shrubs stretching down the middle, owes its existence – and its elegance – to the building of Grand Central Station (*see page 93*). Until then it carried a hideously noisy railroad track, but when the trains went underground the railroad company were able to develop the land around the station. Vibration-proof apartment blocks went up on either side of the Avenue, which quickly gained its exclusive cachet, one that it has not lost, despite the emergence of banks and office blocks in place of the old apartment houses. ② Crouching below **Park Avenue Plaza** is that male-only bastion, the **Racquet and Tennis Club** (McKim, Mead and White, 1918). ③ It is a treat to turn the corner and find the Byzantine-Romanesque bulk of **St Bartholomew's** (Bertram Goodhue, 1919). It sports a splendid Stanford White designed/Vanderbilt financed triple portico, an attractive Community House (1927), a charming little garden, a mosaic of the Transfiguration in the apse, and a massive organ. The church is the setting for afternoon concerts and recitals, also Shakespeare performances. ④ Soaring above St Bart's is the slim tower of the **GE Building**, designed in 1931 to harmonize with the church's attractive, huddled lines. It is embellished with lavish Art Deco detailing. ⑤ The **Waldorf-Astoria**'s twin towers have sheltered an impressive array of famous residents, including Cole Porter, Frank Sinatra, Lucky Luciano and the Duchess of Windsor. The hotel is full of flourish – and shops, restaurants and scurrying people (**\$\$\$**). ⑥ The **Beverly** hotel (125 E 50th St; obscured) has modest suites with kitchenettes (**\$\$**); a rare 24-hour pharmacy, **Kaufman**, is on the premises. ⑦ **Loews Summit** (569 Lexington Ave.; obscured), bland international hotel (**\$\$\$**). ⑧ The criss-cross pattern on **780 Third Ave.**, made by omitting the windows, rings the changes (Skidmore, Owings and Merrill, 1984). ⑨ **Chemcourt** at the Chemical Bank is a particularly verdant glass-enclosed plaza. ⑩ The **Inter-Continental**, with its bronze aviary in the lobby, is a survivor of Park Avenue's elegant 1920s development by the railroad company, when it was called the Barclay (**\$\$\$**). ⑪ Not to be missed, **Caswell-Massey**, pharmacists since 1752 and resident here since the 1920s. The sober fittings and apothecary's bottles remain the same, as do many of the beauty products, which date back to colonial days. ⑫ **Halloran House** hotel (**\$\$\$**).

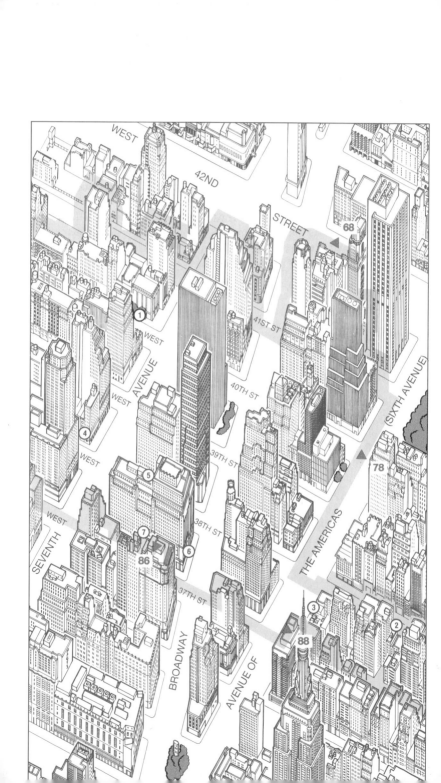

The unexceptional blocks shown here represent another of New York's many changes of face and pace – for a city laid out so monotonously it is remarkable how dramatically its character alters every few streets. This is the Garment Center, home to the rag trade which has been active since l9thC immigrant days and is still the city's main industry. It keeps as many as 300,000 people employed and produces one third of America's clothing, from the cheap and tawdry to the elegant creations of the country's top designers, who are based here. This is very much a working neighborhood, one which becomes eerily deserted after hours. During the day, though, it is worth a rummage round the streets to find strange old shops, catch glimpses of milliners hard at work, and watch the frantic messengers who dash along the sidewalks with bulging racks of clothes in tow. Amongst the shops, look out for: ① **Art-Max** (250 W 40th St; obscured), renowned for its wedding fabrics; ② **Hyman Hendler** (67 W 38th St), wonderful ribbons, tassels and tie-backs, and **Tinsel Trading Co**. (47 W 38th St), with piles of trimmings; ③ **M&J Trimmmings Co**. (1008 Ave. of the Americas), more mounds of mainly Victorian-style trimmings; ④ **William N. Ginsburg** (242 W 38th St; obscured), dressmakers' fabrics. And don't miss ⑤ the **Gordon Button Co**. (142 W 38th St; obscured) for a staggering choice of 5,000 different types of button, including irresistible antique and novelty ones. For refreshment, the workers use ⑥ **Jerusalem 2** (**$**) as a pit-stop. Nearest restaurant proper is ⑦ **Woods 37th** (148 W 37th St; obscured; **$$$**).

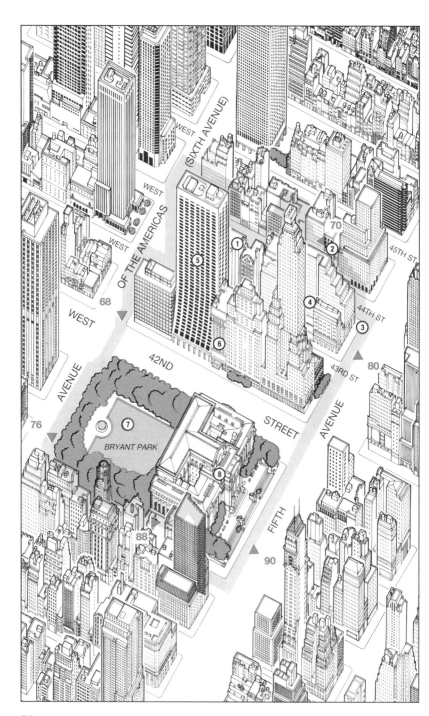

Bryant Park

These Midtown streets around Bryant Park have a staid air but they are punctuated by some noteworthy buildings. ① The **Royalton** (44 W 44th St; obscured) was a down-at-heel hotel until the late Steve Rubell breathed life of the hippest kind into it (**$$$**). Here, in Philippe Starck's striking but soulless space-age interiors the beautiful people meet and partake, amongst other things, of the best tea in town. ② Drop in at the **General Society of Mechanics and Tradesmen** (No. 20; obscured) and wonder at 'A Very Complicated Lock' in their Mossman Lock Collection. Opposite are the splendid Harvard and New York Yacht Clubs, and the Algonquin Hotel (*see page 71*). ③ Check the time by the **Seth Thomas clock**, one of America's few remaining cast-iron sidewalk timepieces. ④ Practically every late 19thC neo-classical flight of fancy in Manhattan was erected by the firm of McKim, Mead and White, and the **Century Club**, the architects' own, is a particularly flattering example, in Palladian mood. ⑤ Architects Skidmore, Owings and Merrill built two identical high-rises for different clients in 1974, this, the **W.R. Grace Building**, and the Solow Building on W 57th Street. Whether you admire the buildings' double-sided slope or not, this one badly breaks up the street wall. ⑥ In 1924 George Gershwin first performed *Rhapsody in Blue*, great Manhattan music, in this building, now the **Graduate Center of New York University**. The ground floor mall (temporary exhibitions) connects 42nd and 43rd Streets. ⑦ In 1853, two years after London's Great Exhibition, New York erected a copycat Crystal Palace which spectacularly burned down five years later. The site is now **Bryant Park**, laid out in the 1930s as a charming formal public garden. It fell into disrepute, a prey to drug pushers, but recent renovation has made Midtown's only open space enjoyable once more. ⑧ **New York Public Library** has terrific presence. A handsome, finely detailed Beaux Arts building (Carrère and Hastings, 1911), it has a pair of famous stone lions, richly marbled and paneled interiors, and over six million reference books stacked beneath Bryant Park.

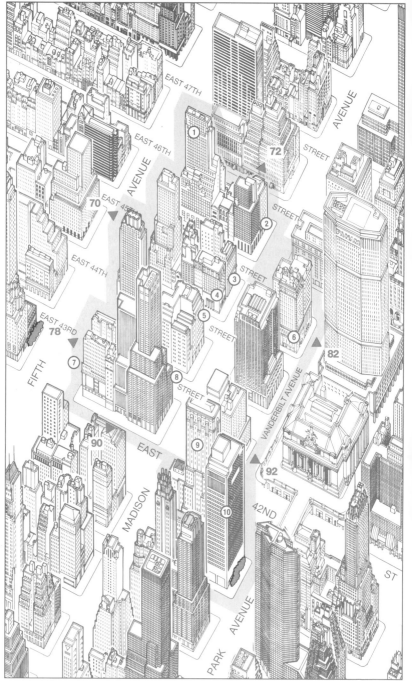

EAST 47TH

EAST 46TH AVENUE

STREET

① 72

AVENUE EAST 45TH STREET

70 ②

STREET

③

④

⑤ STREET

⑥

82

78 ⑦

FIFTH ⑧ STREET

90 ⑨

EAST 43RD

MADISON EAST ⑩

92

VANDERBILT AVENUE

42ND

PARK AVENUE

ST

Fifth Avenue at 42nd Street

① Walking north along Fifth Avenue the eye is attracted by the jolly Egyptianesque faience which decorates the upper floors of the recently overhauled **Fred F. French Building**, a bit of fun along the way. So is the building's lobby, worth a look. ② **F.R. Tripler**, gentlemanly, dead straight menswear store, established 1886. ③ **Paul Stuart**, more menswear, very British, very stylish. ④ Menswear again, this time for the inimitable preppy look – Oxford cloth shirts, silk rep ties, plaid shorts, flannel pyjamas, terry cloth bathrobes, topsider shoes and the like – at **Brooks Brothers**. America's oldest mens' clothing store (est. 1818) is now owned by British company Marks and Spencer, and its wares are surprisingly affordable. ⑤ Also well-priced are the classic range of mens' shoes at **Fellman Ltd** opposite, (24 E 44th St; obscured). ⑥ Facing the Pan Am building, and looking fairly disapproving about it, is the **Yale Club**. Notice the plaque concerning the fate of one Nathan Hale, Revolutionary hero and old Yalie. "I only regret that I have but one life to lose for my country." ⑦ Another splendidly renovated interior, this time at the neo-Renaissance **Israel Discount Bank** (511 5th Ave.; obscured). ⑧ Two oddities in E 43rd Street: on the south side, the **Chemical Bank**, No. 4, standing alone, has a medieval Italian air, while on the north side, the **Church of Christ Scientist** seems crushed by its own massive pillared portico and mocked by the perfectly ordinary apartment block that sits on top of it. ⑨ When the 53-story **Lincoln Building** was built in 1929, its owners boasted: "No other structure has ever been created where clean, fresh air is more abundant or where radiant sunlight is more plentiful". ⑩ The construction of the adjacent **Philip Morris Building** in 1982 finally put paid to that. Its first floor houses an outpost of the **Whitney Museum of American Art** (*see page 45*).

EAST

EAST

49TH

72

48TH ST

AVENUE

74

MADISON

3

AVENUE

2

4

1

80

AVENUE

LEXINGTON

94

VANDERBILT

92

AVENUE

THIRD

EAST

AVE

42ND

PARK

STREET

Pan Am Building

Walking south along Park Avenue, the great bland wall of the Pan Am Building looming over the hapless Helmsley and totally obliterating the route ahead, is one of the city's most memorable sights. Boorish interloper it undoubtedly is, but a magnetic one all the same, especially when the Helmsley is dramatically floodlit at night. ① The **Pan Am Building**'s 2.4 million square feet of office space was unprecedented at the time (1963), as was its pre-cast concrete curtain wall. Its best bit is the rear balcony (walk straight through the main hall from the E 45th Street entrance) which overlooks Grand Central Station's beautiful main concourse (*see page 93*). ② Now the **Helmsley Building**, this was designed in 1929 by Warren and Wetmore, architects of Grand Central Station, as the headquarters of the railroad company. It boldly straddled Park Avenue, necessitating two road tunnels (and two pedestrian ones) so that traffic could pass right through. They are still in use. Appropriately for the Helmsleys, gold is the building's theme, both inside and out. ③ **The Roosevelt**, once popular for its proximity to the then brand new station, is today a down-to-earth hotel patronized by visiting businessmen (**$$**). ④ Two fat, slug-like black tubes, intertwined, rotate very slowly by means of solar power in Lowell Jones' sculpture, *Performance Machine* (1986; obscured).

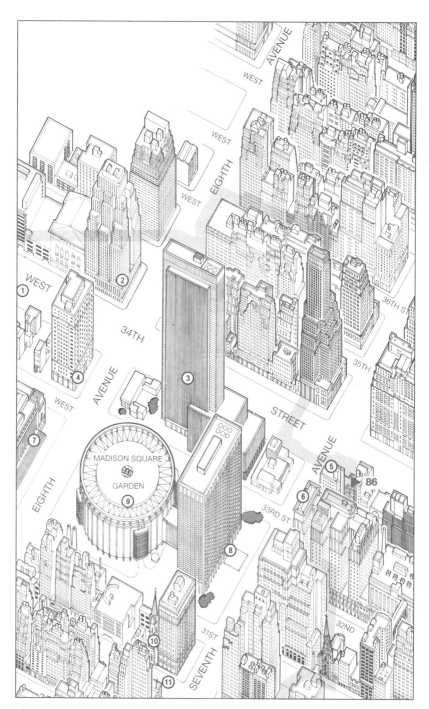

Madison Square Garden

① **Sloane House YMCA**. ② **No. 481 8th Ave** is a quirky piece of '30s architecture. Formerly the New York Hotel, it had 2,500 rooms. In contrast ③ **One Penn Plaza** is a typical '70s vertical slab. ④ **T.S. Ma**, a reliable Chinese in an area not noted for its restaurants. ⑤ **J.J. Applebaum's**, a huge, bright deli on two floors (**$**). ⑥ The **New York Penta Hotel** (**$$**), favoured by delegates attending the Jacob Javits Convention Center to the west (off map). ⑦ Like the unremarkable Penta, the **General Post Office** (read the famous inscription on the façade) is another product of those ubiquitous architects McKim, Mead and White, this one in 1913. It matched their *tour de force* which stood opposite, ⑧ **Penn Station**. Of all the architectural disasters perpetrated on New York, the destruction of the neoclassical Pennsylvania Station is deemed by many the worst, not least because its replacement was so lackluster. This consists of an office complex on top of a warren for the station, and ⑨ **Madison Square Garden Center**. This is the fourth version of the famous sports and exhibition complex on the third site (the first two were at Madison Square, hence the name). Underlining the waste, it is due to move yet again, and the present stadium will be demolished. ⑩ It is always a pleasure to stumble across a serene old church in a busy New York street, and **St John's** (RC) is one of the nicest surprises. Its slender brownstone exterior encases an exquisite interior of radiant white marble. ⑪ Between 28th and 31st Streets west of 7th Avenue is the **Fur District**, with such showrooms as Birger Christensen (150 W 30th St), Antonovich (333 7th Ave.) and Golden-Feldman (345 7th Ave.; 12th floor).

Herald Square

① **Nelson Tower**, a 1930s office block decorated with a period bas-relief sculpture at its top. ② **Crossland Savings Bank**, masquerading as an Ancient Greek temple (1924). ③ **Herald Square** is in fact, like ④ **Greeley Square** to the south, a small triangle besieged by traffic, beset by vagrants and ignored by passers-by. Both their names recall the days when New York's major newspapers had their headquarters here. The *New York Herald*, run by James Gordon Bennett (the man who sent Stanley to find Livingstone) had its headquarters in a magnificent McKim, Mead and White *palazzo*. The building's splendid clock still survives in the square. Take a look at it when the hour strikes. Horace Greeley (statue) was the founder of the *New York Tribune*. The arrival of the likes of Bennett and Greeley put an end to Herald Square's former and much shadier reputation as the heart of the notorious Tenderloin district where dance halls, bars and brothels crammed together hard up against the slums of Hell's Kitchen to the west (*see page 43*). ⑤ It is appropriate that **Macy's**, 'the world's largest department store' should be located so close to the Garment Center (*see page 77*), where much of its merchandise is created. It stocks much more than its huge selection of fashions though: best of all is the basement 'Cellar' with a food market and excellent selection of kitchenware. Whether you will ever find what you are looking for, or find your way out again before nightfall, is another matter. ⑥ **The Herald Center** is a run-of-the-mill shopping mall, albeit an upright one, but its glass elevators are fun for a ride. ⑦ Formerly Gimbel's, this is now the Manhattan branch of Brooklyn's largest department store Abraham & Straus: **A&S Plaza**. Notice the connecting bridge above W 32nd Street.

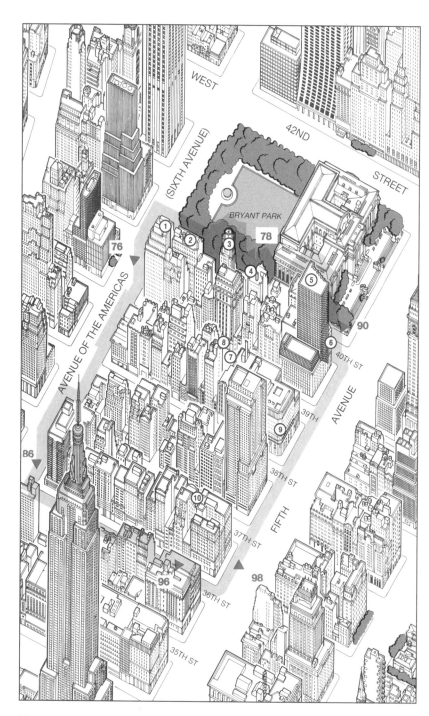

Fifth Avenue at Lord and Taylor

West 40th Street bordering Bryant Park provides a dramatic panorama of some of the city's most interesting skyscrapers. ① The open park to the north and double-height windows flood light into the flamboyant Beaux **Arts Bryant Park Studios** (Charles A. Rich, 1901). ② Colossal Tuscan columns flank the entrance to the old **Republican Club** (1904), now Daytop Village Inc., World Federation of Therapeutic Communities. ③ Jewel in the crown of West 40th Street's skyscrapers is Raymond Hood's sensational black and gold **American Standard Building**, a fusion of Art Deco design and Gothic detail, built in 1923 for the American Radiator Company. When illuminated at night, it has been likened – appropriately for a heating company – to a glowing coal. ④ Built as the **Engineers Club** in 1906, now converted to apartments, 32 West 40th Street (obscured) is a well-proportioned Renaissance Revival building, with Corinthian columns that echo the New York Public Library (*see page 79*) opposite. ⑤ The glass curtain wall of the angular **Republic National Bank Tower** (1986) makes an anachronistic backdrop to ⑥ the opulent neoclassical **Knox Hat Building**, built in 1902 for a prestigious hatter. Dotted about the **streets below West 40th**, on the periphery of one of Manhattan's seediest areas, are distinctive little shops, selling every Garment Center requisite from buttons and braids to sequins and rhinestones. **39th Street** boasts a number of good restaurants; all typical of the Garment Center (*see page 77*), lively at lunchtime, dead at dinner. They include ⑦ the fun, informal Italian **Grappino** (No. 38; obscured; **$$**), ⑧ **Sunny East**, an up-market Szechuan restaurant (**$$**), with an impressive fish tank. ⑨ **Lord and Taylor**. The department store that has its roots in a little dry goods shop set up by an English immigrant in 1826. It moved to its present location in 1914 and still has a genteel air. Classic American designer fashion for women and men, shoes and housewares are its strengths, and people will travel from the other side of the city to see its Christmas windows, painstakingly decorated with snow scenes. ⑩ If in search of an anchor, a jib or simply a pair of docksiders, **Goldberg's Marine Distributors** (12 W 37th St; obscured) is the place to go.

East of Bryant Park

Quiet streets, these, some with splendid views westwards of the great New York Public Library (*see page 79*). ① If you like Californian wine, choose from the huge selection at the confusingly named **Park Avenue Liquor Shop**. ② **Lloyd and Haig** (295 Madison Ave; obscured), traditional men's shoe store. ③ **Délices de France** (289 Madison Ave.; obscured), *chocolatier* with a French-style grill above (**$**). ④ Look up at the jewel-bright oranges, greens and blues of the little mosaic ceiling in the lobby of **No. 274** Madison Ave. ⑤ Have your shoes transformed, or merely repaired, at cobblers **T.O. Dey** (No. 9). ⑥ Notice the row of attractive **brownstones** mid-block on E 39th St. No. 28 is the **C.G. Jung Center**. ⑦ **Doral Park Avenue**. Into Murray Hill, a good hotel of considerable yet unostentatious comfort, with a fitness center attached (**$$$**).

EAST VANDERBILT AVENUE

EAST

EAST

80

82

AVENUE

AVENUE

44TH ST

43RD ST

94

90

42ND

STREET

LEXINGTON

41ST

40TH ST

39TH ST

38TH ST

THIRD

100

102

①
②
③
④
⑤
⑥
⑦

Grand Central Station/Chrysler Building

Besieged on all fronts by towering, mostly characterless office buildings, **Grand Central Station** is a Beaux Arts masterpiece that has withstood the onslaught. Its impressive classical façade, complete with triumphal arches flanked by Doric columns and surmounted by a Jules Coutan sculpture, surveys the length of Park Avenue to the south. Eclipsing formidable rivals McKim, Mead and White in a competition, architects Reed and Stem, with associates Warren and Wetmore, also designed a highly complex network of subterranean tracks beneath their magnificent terminal building. Outside the 42nd Street entrance, shoeshine boys – relics of the '20s – tout for business. Inside, the spacious Main Concourse is an imposing sight, with its marble floor and walls and soaring dark vaulted ceiling, decorated with stars and symbols. New York's most famous seafood restaurant, **The Oyster Bar** (**$$**) is located in the bowels of the station. A noisy, cavernous, no frills place, with tiled walls and arched ceiling, it is a great institution, but the plain dishes don't often live up to their reputation. ② There are few more spectacular night sights in New York than that Art Deco triumph, the **Chrysler Building**, the arches of its radiator-grill spire lit up by fluorescent light. Even by day it looks dramatic, stainless steel glinting in the sun. Built in 1930 for the famous motor company and fleetingly the world's tallest building, it is decorated with subtle representations of cars and their parts. ③ A joke of a skyscraper, **425 Lexington Avenue** is a post-modern aquamarine and glass affair, decorated with pink marble. ④ Romanesque-style **Bowery Savings Bank**, its dark sculpted façade dominated by a monumental arch. Try to see the vast and sumptuously decorated banking hall and lobby, with its elevator doors of beaten brass and a blue and gold ceiling. ⑤ **Chanin Building**, a flamboyant piece of Art Deco built in 1929 for the real estate company, with a wonderful swirling bas-relief in terracotta by Edward Trumbull at the third story. Peek into the lobby for a glimpse of the remarkable convector grilles. ⑥ **101 Park Avenue**, a contorted black glass high-rise office building, containing **C.I. Ristorante** (**$$**), which hosts live jazz on Wednesday and Thursday evenings in a high-tech setting. ⑦ The 1955 **Mobil Building**, clad in panels of a highly economic embossed stainless steel which create air streams that keep the building clean.

West of the UN/Ford Foundation

① **Roger Smith Winthrop** (501 Lexington Ave.; obscured; **$$**), a recently upgraded middle-of-the-road Midtown hotel. ② **Nanni**, long-established (more than 20 years, which is long by New York standards) Italian with cramped seating, gently fading decor and delicious pastas – but the prices are high (**$$$**). ③ In pale stone and very pale brick is **St Agnes** rectory (obscured), and, next door, the red-brick church itself, impressive if rather dilapidated. ④ Gangster Paul Castellano met his end in a customary hail of bullets outside **Sparks** (210 E 46th St; obscured; **$$$**), a popular steakhouse noted not so much for its steaks as for its all-encompassing wine list. Nearby, ⑤ the **Pen and Pencil** (205 E 45th St; obscured; **$$**) is another steakhouse. This time the slabs of beef are served in old-fashioned premises with a genteel, clubby air. ⑥ **Palm** and, opposite, **Palms Too** (**$$$**) where foreigners love to come and see what American-size steaks and lobsters are all about – answer: mammoth. Apart from the no-nonsense food, the service is brusque, there is sawdust on the floor, caricatures on the walls and a clamorous din. ⑦ For a change of scene and a spell of peace and quiet you can do no better than to step into the philanthropic **Ford Foundation**'s lush, ever-changing indoor garden, complete with pool and stream. This was New York's first and best atrium (Roche, Dinkeloo and Assocs, 1967), an elegant 12-story glass greenhouse supported by four granite columns. It must rate as one of the most pleasant buildings in the city in which to work. ⑧ Here are the **steps** which approach ⑨ **Tudor City Place**, the overhead street that spans E 42nd Street (*see Tudor City, page 103*). Also visible is the most northerly of Tudor City's two private parks. From Tudor City Place there is a sweeping view of the United Nations.

BROADWAY

(SIXTH AVENUE)

EAST

AVENUE OF THE AMERICAS

34TH

STREET

37TH ST

36TH ST

35TH ST

33RD ST

32ND ST

31ST ST

86

88

98

108

106

①
②
③
④
⑤
⑥
⑦
⑧
⑨

Empire State Building

An area dominated by the doyenne of New York skyscrapers, and for 41 years the world's tallest, ① the **Empire State Building**. Its geometric tempered Art Deco design, depicted on thousands of postcards, evokes memories of '30s movies, Gershwin music and the unforgettable King Kong, clinging to its spire. The most distinctive element in Manhattan's famous skyline was built on the site of the original Waldorf-Astoria, a turn-of-the-century society watering-place, which comprised two connecting hotels, built by warring relatives, Mrs William Astor and her nephew William Waldorf Astor. During the Depression few firms could afford office space in the Empire State, and it was nicknamed the Empty State Building. Taxes were paid out of money made by the open observation deck, subsequently caged in to prevent suicides. Every February there is a race up the 1,575 steps to the 86th floor, usually in a heart-stopping 12 minutes. The **Guinness World Exhibit Hall** is on concourse level. ② Typical 19thC Garment District bar, **Keen's Steak and Chop House** (72 W 36th St; obscured) serves wonderfully succulent chops. ③ Playwright Eugene O'Neill lived at **36 West 35th Street** from 1921 to 1922. ④ When the *beau monde* resided in Murray Hill, the place for faithless husbands to buy baubles for their mistresses, or peace offerings for their wives, was **Gorham's**, the jewelers, which occupied this once-splendid McKim, Mead and White *palazzo*, later altered unsympathetically. ⑤ A 1930s delight, now marred by 1990s store fronts, which originally housed **Spear & Co**. furniture store (22 W 34th St; obscured). ⑥ In a 'riches to rags' story, Henry J. Hardenbergh's extravagant Beaux Arts mansion (1897) at one stage became a shelter for the homeless; now it is the **Hotel Martinique**, undergoing restoration (**$$**). ⑦ **Henry Westpfal** (4 E 32nd St; obscured), a gigantic pair of scissors above the entrance gives a clue to the wares of this delightfully old-fashioned craft tool shop, which opened in 1874. ⑧ If you cannot guess from the inscriptions dotted about the classical façade and the interlocking initials on the wrought-iron balconies, this was the *Life* magazine building, now **Hotel Clinton** (**$$**). ⑨ **Kaskel & Kaskel Building**, crumbling exponent of the Beaux Arts genre.

Murray Hill

The spot where Robert Murray chose to build his farm in the 1750s had become one of the most fashionable addresses by the end of the 19thC, and remains a sedate residential district to this day. Its streets, many still lined with elegant brownstones, lend themselves to a leisurely stroll. ① Before its younger sibling, the Royalton (*see page 79*), usurped its position, **Morgan's** (237 Madison Ave.; obscured) was New York's hippest hotel. Monochrome and minimalist, it was conceived by the late Steve Rubell, of Studio 54 fame, and designed by Andre Putnam (**$$$**). ② **DeLamar Mansion**, now the Polish Consulate, Beaux Arts extravaganza, built by C.P.H. Gilbert in 1905 for a Dutch seaman and mining magnate in a bid to outdo his rival opposite, J.P. Morgan. ③ Choose between a genuine *tatami* suite, complete with futon and hot tub, or a chintzy Colonial-style room at the Japanese-owned **Kitano** (**$$**). ④ **J.P. Morgan Jr House**, a once magnificent brownstone, now owned by the Lutheran Church and sadly dilapidated, though plans are afoot to restore and incorporate it into the Morgan Library. ⑤ Bow-fronted neo-Georgian **Union League Club**, founded in the 19thC by a band of Republicans who left the Union Club in a huff because it refused to drum out Confederate supporters. ⑥ Half a day in the **Pierpoint Morgan Library** will restore the spirit of the most jaded sightseer. In a McKim, Mead and White palazzo are J.P.'s superb collection of Flemish Books of Hours, eclectic drawings, letters and scores, a galleried library with two concealed staircases, and his study, where he kept his 'knicknacks'. ⑦ **H. Percy Silver Parish House** (209 Madison Ave.; obscured), charming 1868 townhouse, named for a vicar of ⑧ the Episcopal **Church of the Incarnation**. Its blackened exterior lends it a sinister air, but don't be deterred, it contains some stunning Tiffany glass. ⑨ **Complete Traveller** (199 Madison Ave.; obscured). Ring the bell to be admitted to a little shop, brimming with books about places as distant and diverse as Alaska and the Alps. ⑩ McKim, Mead and White **Collectors' Club** (22 E 35th St; obscured). ⑪ A plaque marks the site of **Murray Farm** and commemorates Mrs Murray's courageous role in the American Revolution. ⑫ Congenial Italian café with sidewalk tables, **Dolci on the Park** (**$$**).

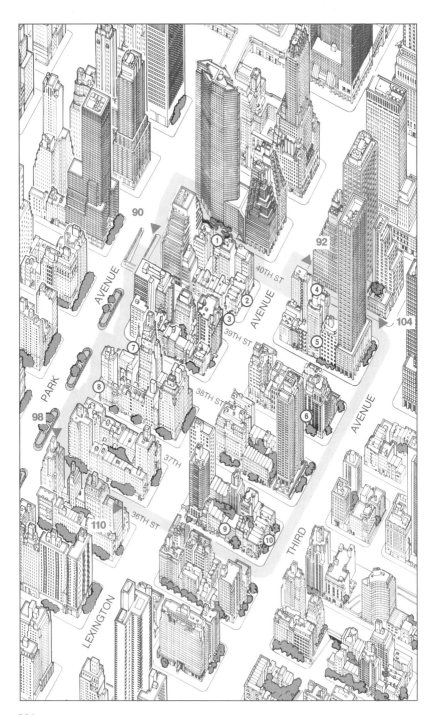

East of Murray Hill

① The **Bedford** (No. 118; obscured), with a wood-paneled lobby and an unexpected exterior buzzing with figures of old men, griffins, owls, and strange mythological creatures, is a mid-price hotel with kitchenettes in every room (**$$**). ② **Christine's**. Filling Polish fare – *borscht, pierogis, blintzes* – in simple surroundings (pink tablecloths, chrome chairs); always popular (**$**). Next door is **Porteroz**, a neighborhood favorite for its good value northern Italian cooking (**$$**). ③ Two excellent hotels in this stretch of E 39th St (both obscured): the **Doral Court** (No. 130; **$$**) and its more grown-up sister the **Doral Tuscany** (No. 118; **$$$**). Both are calm, civilized and good on extra touches. Both have pleasant restaurants, the airy **Courtyard Café** in the former, and the more serious **Time and Again** in the latter. Opposite the Doral Court is **Maison Japonaise** (No. 125), a smart Franco/Japanese restaurant, as the name implies (**$$**). ④ Alone and neglected, **No. 148** is an endearingly handsome carriage house dating from 1875. One wonders what will become of it. ⑤ In 1920 Scott Fitzgerald lived here at **No. 145** when it was a hotel. Soon afterwards he began his ill-fated marriage to Zelda. ⑥ Another touching carriage house, this one seemingly transplanted from an Amsterdam canalside, **No. 149**. Opposite, **No. 152** (obscured) is enchanting, a quaint little shuttered house, mid-19thC, set back behind a pretty paved garden, full of ivy. Across the front, a stone loggia (notice the dolphins) lends the house its air of exclusivity. ⑦ **No. 57 Park Avenue** (obscured) is an eye-catching Beaux Arts confection. Next door is the architecturally much less uplifting **Church of St Saviour** (RC). ⑧ Understated luxury, Park Avenue style, at the **Sheraton Park Avenue** hotel (**$$$**). ⑨ A pretty row of **brownstones**, typical of Murray Hill. ⑩ If you need feeding in the middle of the night, head for **Sarge's** deli, because it is open 24 hours a day (**$**).

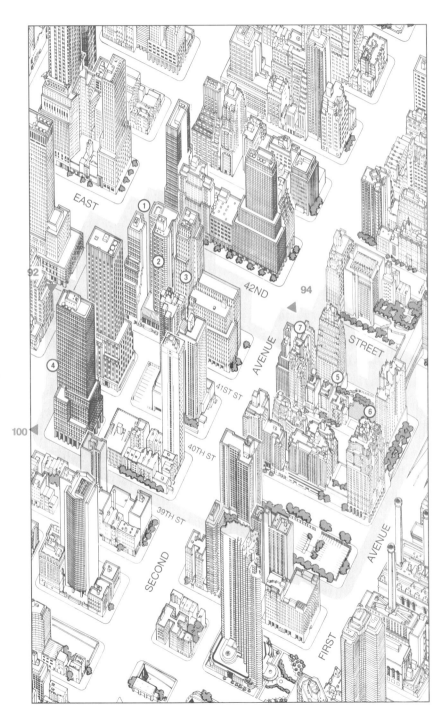

East 42nd Street

That great east-west artery, 42nd Street, which slices Midtown in half, here reaches the East River. Its line-up of impressive buildings continues all the way, culminating with the Ford Foundation (*see page 95*) and the United Nations (*see page 105*). ① The last **Horn and Hardat automat** (200 E 42nd St; obscured; **$**), sole survivor of a once-flourishing species, closed in April 1991. These waiterless restaurants, where individual portions of food sat glumly behind rows and rows of little glass and chrome doors to be unlocked 'automatically' by the insertion of a nickel or a dime, were a wonderful novelty during the Depression years. This one was built as an afterthought in 1958. ② **New York Helmsley**, efficient hotel geared to business people (**$$$**). ③ The **Daily News Building** is an early high-rise (Howells and Hood, 1930), with an impressive matching 1958 addition. Step into the lobby to see the revolving globe. ④ Drop in for a quick dozen oysters at **Dock's Oyster Bar**, or stay longer for one of their excellent fried seafood dishes (633 3rd Ave.; obscured; **$$**). ⑤ The **Church of the Covenant** was built in 1871, but lies within the later Tudor City complex. It has a pretty interior with bright stained glass windows. ⑥ For a sightseer just strolling by, **Tudor City** comes as a curious puzzle. A residential enclave built entirely in Tudor style in the mid-1920s by the prominent Fred F. French property company, it was conceived to stand aloof from the then grim and murky streets below. The apartment buildings were designed to face on to their own two private parks; notice that east-facing walls are almost windowless. The development, still aloof, includes shops, a post office and a hotel, formerly the Tudor, now the modest ⑦ **Chatwal Inn** (304 E 42nd St; **$**); *see also page 95*.

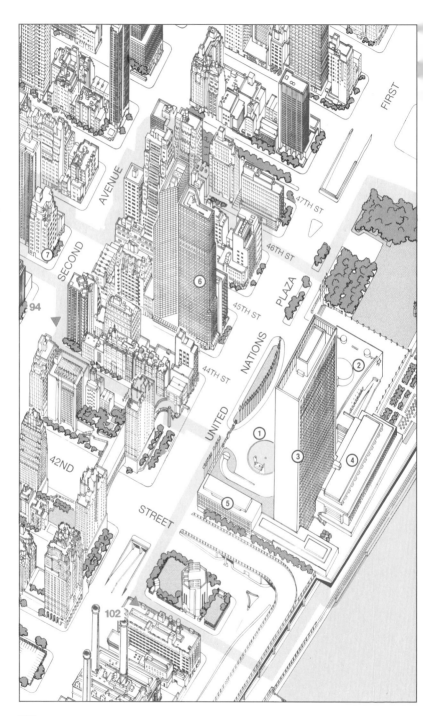

FIRST

AVENUE

SECOND

47TH ST

46TH ST

PLAZA

45TH ST

UNITED NATIONS

44TH ST

42ND

STREET

⑦

94

⑥

①

②

③

④

⑤

102

United Nations Headquarters

The best thing about a visit to ① the **United Nations** is the buffet lunch (weekdays only) at the **Delegates' Dining Room** (**$$**) on the top floor of the Conference Building overlooking East River. Once fortified, you could take one of the frequent guided tours, or better still, attend an open session of the General Assembly or Security Council (free tickets from information desk). The UN Headquarters were designed in the 1950s by a committee of international architects (including Le Corbusier who later withdrew), and comprise ② the **General Assembly Building**, ③ the slab-like **Secretariat Building**, ④ the **Conference Building** (which includes three splendid Council Chambers donated by Scandinavia), and ⑤ the **Hammerskjold Library**. Outside the General Assembly Building, flags of all the member nations fly in alphabetical order, which is how delegates are seated inside. Yet despite the UN's importance, never more so than today, despite the flags, the works of art donated by each nation, the tranquil gardens, the superb riverside setting, it is hard to feel a sense of awe here – the place is rather dull. It was built on land – warehouses and tenements – bought and donated by John D. Rockerfeller. In earlier, rural times there was a bay, a creek and a farm here all by the name of Turtle. This area is still called Turtle Bay (don't miss **Turtle Bay Gardens**, the lovely row houses with communal garden on E 49th and E 48th Streets between 2nd and 3rd Avenues, off map) and the river still flows beneath E 48th Street. ⑥ Opposite the UN rises a pair of visually dizzying skyscrapers, **1 and 2 United Nations Plaza** (1976 and 1980), their green glass curtain walls criss-crossed with aluminum to resemble giant sheets of graph paper. The 28th floor of No. 1 is the lobby of the **United Nations Plaza** hotel (**$$$**); its **Ambassador's Grill** (amazing mirrored ceiling) serves excellent Gascon cuisine (**$$**).

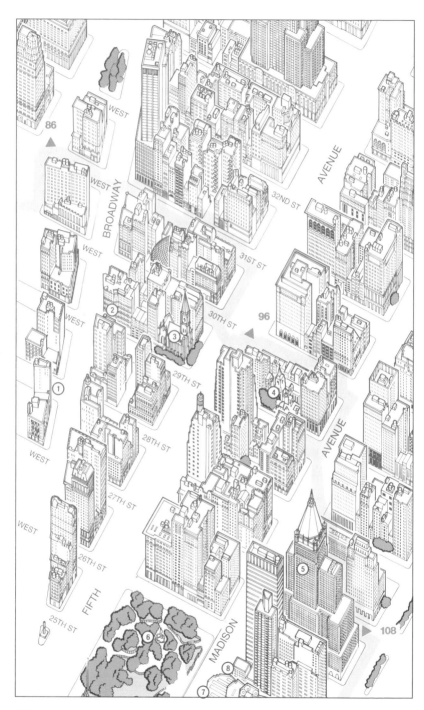

Madison Square Park

(1) Where was Tin Pan Alley? It was here, along **W 28th Street**, where scores of songwriters toiled to feed the musical theaters that had sprung up along the length of Broadway. Now the theater district has contracted to the area around Times Square (*see page 69*), but in the early years of the century theaters, lavish hotels, fashionable stores and restaurants lined 'the Great White Way'. Most of these buildings are either sad reminders, or have disappeared altogether. One exception is (2) **Gilsey House**, then a noted hotel, now apartments. In those days, striped awnings at all the windows gave the cast-iron and marble building even more of a festive air. (3) Calm and dignified, the **Marble Collegiate Church** dates from 1854, but its Dutch Reform congregation has existed since 1628, when New York was the Dutch colony of Nieuw Amsterdam. (4) The story of how the **Church of the Transfiguration** became known as the 'Little Church Around the Corner' bears repeating. When an actor, George Holland, died in 1870, his friend Joseph Jefferson tried to have him buried at a local church. The pastor refused, but told him "There's a little church around the corner that will help you." The church, which has an enchanting feel, continues to this day to have strong links with both the acting profession and the needy. (5) Instantly recognizable by its square tower topped by a gilded conical hat, the **New York Life Building** (1928) boasts an impressively ornate lobby. It stands on the site of the first and second Madison Square Gardens, the latter designed by Stanford White, of the great architectural firm of McKim, Mead and White. Here, sitting in the roof garden, he met a sensational end – shot by the jealous husband of a former lover, Evelyn Nesbitt. (6) **Madison Square Park** was the focal point of this once fashionable area, but now it is simply a welcome oasis, filled with statuary. (7) The 700ft clock tower of the **Metropolitan Life Insurance Company** (off map). Built in 1909, it was inspired by the *campanile* of St Mark's, Venice, and was then the world's tallest building – for a while. (8) **Appellate Division, NYS Supreme Court** (35 E 25th St; obscured). A fine stately home of a building, both inside and out (1900).

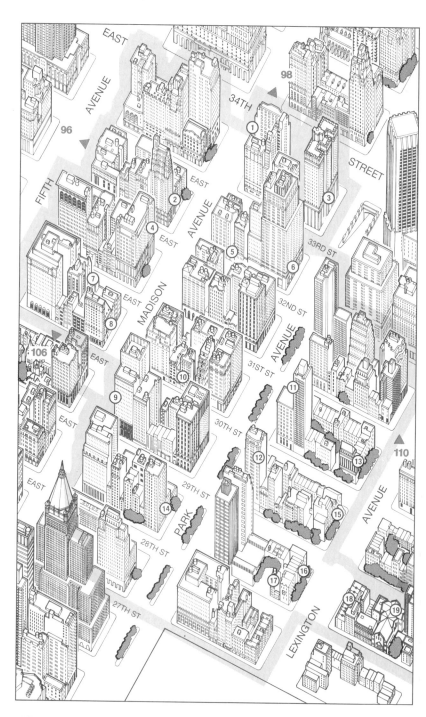

Park Avenue South

① **Salta in Bocca** (179 Madison Ave.; obscured) is a dependable Italian restaurant (**$$**). ② Andy Warhol's offices and studio were housed in **The Factory**, a deceptive sliver of a building, which stretches back in an L-shape to 32nd Street and sports huge studio windows on its two façades. ③ A Warren and Wetmore building, which was once the **Vanderbilt Hotel**. ④ A fusion of Art Nouveau and Gothic detail in Frank Goodwillie's **Remsen Building** (1917). ⑤ Handsome brownstone mansion built in 1895 for the **Grolier Club**. ⑥ **No. 2 Park Avenue**, a blaze of brightly colored Art Deco tiles decorate the top of this otherwise sedate office building. Also home to Larry Forgione's **An American Place**, where the fare is traditional American, but the setting suave and spacious (**$$$**). ⑦ A treat lies in store in the shape of **Madison Avenue Baptist Church Parish House** (30 31st St;obscured), a delightful early 20thC brick and limestone Romanesque building, decorated with Arabic motifs. ⑧ McKim, Mead and White's Federal-style **American Academy of Dramatic Arts**, built for the Colony Club in 1905. ⑨ The exuberant Renaissance-style **Emmet Building** (1912). ⑩ Lovers of Lebanese cuisine, look no further than **Cedars of Lebanon** (39 E 30th St; obscured; **$**). ⑪ 1970s rusted steel **Raymond R. Corbett Building** (451 Park Ave.; obscured), named for an iron-workers' union leader. ⑫ **Bowker Building** (1929), eccentric in its architecture and variety of colors. ⑬ A splendid classical 'temple', built in 1909 as the **New York School of Applied Design for Women**, now the Vocational Rehabilitation Agency. ⑭ For authentic French bistro food, try **Park Bistro** (**$$**). ⑮ **First Moravian Church**, built in 1845 in an unpretentious version of the Romanesque. ⑯ **Sonia Rose**, a little restaurant with a lot of atmosphere and a varied menu (**$$**). ⑰ Dynamic American artist Mark Rothko lived at **29 E 28th Street** from 1940 to 1943. ⑱ **No. 123 Lexington Avenue**, inhabited between 1900 and 1907 by newspaper magnate, William Randolph Hearst. ⑲ James Renwick Jr's **St Stephen's Church** (1854), in Romanesque style, which contains a remarkable mural by the Italian artist Constantino Brumidi, who spent 25 years painting the interior of the Capitol in Washington.

South of Murray Hill

From the opulent mansions that line Park Avenue down streets of pretty brownstones, increasingly dilapidated as you travel east, Murray Hill degenerates into seamy Second Avenue. ① In contrast to its pale Park Avenue neighbors, the dark brown brick and stone façade of **J. Hampton Robb Mansion** is an arresting sight. Built by Stanford White at the end of the 19thC in the grand Italian Renaissance style for Robb, a wealthy lawyer and parks commissioner, it now contains luxury condos. ② Dwarfing the only complete row of original brownstones (Nos 105-121) in Murray Hill, the magnificent limestone and brick Beaux Arts **James F.D. Lanier Residence** (1903). ③ Providing a nice break in the row houses, **New Church (Swedenborgian)** (112 E 35th St; obscured) is a low Italianate building, with peeling white paint and a pretty tree-filled garden. ④ A charming backwater, tucked away from the hustle and bustle, **Sniffen Court** is a flagstone-paved mews of ten Romanesque-style stables, built by local builder John Sniffen in the 1850s and converted into houses in the '20s. At the back stands the wall of sculptress Malvina Hoffman's former studios, bearing white relief plaques of horsemen. ⑤ Converted carriage houses at **Nos 155, 157, 158** (obscured) and **159 E 35th Street** with an interesting terracotta frieze. ⑥ **Health Education Center**, uncompromising angled redbrick high-rise, looming above Irving Marantz's Obelisk to Peace (obscured). ⑦ **Armenian Evangelical Church** (152 E 34th St; obscured) has an attractive neo-classical façade and a crude mural on the west wall. ⑧ No. 1 Park Avenue, 1920s building on the site of a 19thC glue factory, later converted to barns for horses. ⑨ **Back Porch** (**$$**), jolly café with a striped awning and tables outside; a perfect watering-place on a hot day. ⑩ **Milton Glaser Design Studio** (1910). Isolated when its neighbors were demolished, a narrow townhouse – just two windows wide – with an ornate French Renaissance façade is home to one of New York's most prominent designers. ⑪ Quaint and inviting, **Murray Hill Antiques Center Inc**. is cluttered with bric-à-brac and furniture. ⑫ In a pretty ivy-covered brownstone, **Marchi's** (**$$**) a time-honored Italian restaurant with a set menu.

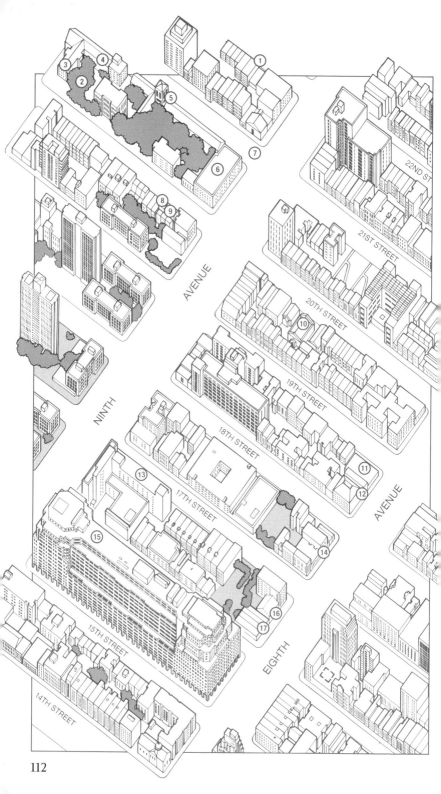

Chelsea

Trees and tenements, factories and fine houses stand cheek-by-jowl in the suburb that was Captain Thomas Clarke's 18thC estate. ① Nos 400-412 West 22nd Street are well-preserved Italianate townhouses (1856), known as **James N. Wells Row. No. 436** (off map), 1835 Greek Revival house, bought by actor Edwin Forrest (*see East Village, page 121*) as a refuge from his overbearing in-laws. ② Sanctuary from the city bustle is assured in the shaded lawns of the **General Theological Seminary** (Haight, 1883-1900). Important components are ③ **West Building** (1835), an early example of the Greek Revival style; ④ **Hoffman Hall**, its reproduction medieval dining hall, complete with musicians' gallery and barrel-vaulted roof; ⑤ **Chapel of the Good Shepherd**, with its dazzling bronze doors and square bell tower, a copy of the one at Magdalen College, Oxford; and ⑥ **St Mark's Library** (1960), the nation's principal collection of ecclesiastical books. ⑦ **West 21st Street** offers a glimpse of old Chelsea in its elegant Italianate houses, set back from the road; their small but verdant front gardens contained behind wrought-iron railings. ⑧ **Cushman Row** of Greek Revival houses, rich in architectural detail, from the cast-iron pineapples on top of the newel posts to the wreaths around the attic windows, built by dry-goods merchant, Don Alonzo Cushman, *en route* to making his fortune. ⑨ **No. 404**, Chelsea's oldest house. In a street of more unspoilt Greek Revival houses, are ⑩ **St Peter's Church**, an early example of Gothic Revival, its spare Greek Revival **Rectory** and Victorian Gothic parish hall, now **Apple Core Theater**, all surrounded by 18thC railings from Trinity Church, Broadway. ⑪ Splendidly restored Art Deco **Joyce Theater**. ⑫ Minimalist bistro, serving tasty French regional food, **Man Ray ($$)**. ⑬ Extraordinary 1960s sloping white tiled building dotted with portholes, built as the **National Maritime Union**. ⑭ An old speakeasy, **Chelsea Place** conceals, beyond an antique shop, a charming and quaint Italian restaurant, with a garden, duck pond, and an upstairs jazz bar **($$)**. ⑮ Massive original 1930s **Port of New York Authority Commerce Building**. ⑯ Simple, homey **Miss Ruby's Café**, with wood floor and warm pink walls, offers a different regional American cuisine every few weeks **($$)**. ⑰ **Cajun** mixes large portions of robust Cajun food with live Dixieland jazz **($$)**.

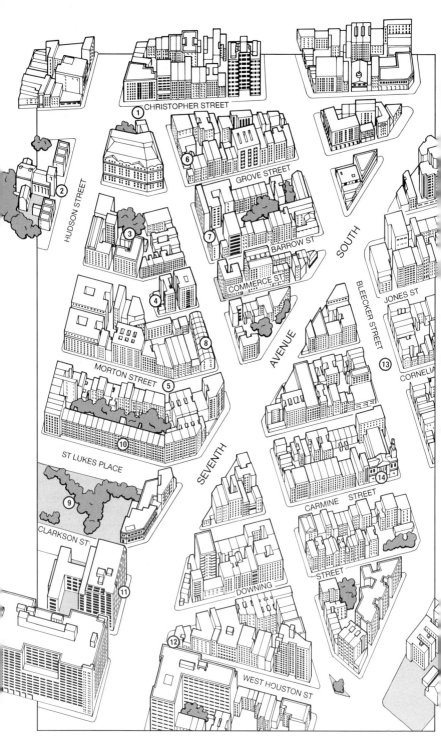

CHRISTOPHER STREET

HUDSON STREET

GROVE STREET

BARROW ST

COMMERCE ST.

SOUTH

AVENUE

BLEECKER STREET

JONES ST

CORNELIA

MORTON STREET

SEVENTH

ST LUKES PLACE

CLARKSON ST

CARMINE STREET

DOWNING

STREET

WEST HOUSTON ST

Greenwich Village/Morton Street

Greenwich Village has been in turns an Indian settlement, a country village, a refuge from plague, a fashionable address, and by the turn of this century, Bohemia. Nowadays chic and wealthy residents rub shoulders with students, street people and tourists. It remains perhaps the most accessible area of Manhattan for visitors, where the work ethic is less in evidence. It is a pretty town within a city, charming by day, alive at night, with a network of little streets that defy the logic of the grid. ① **Christopher Street**, notable in the 1960s as New York's first gay area. Amongst the shops, kitsch, sweet-smelling **Li-Lac** sells home-made chocolates, while one sniff of **McNulty's Tea and Coffee Co**. will draw you inside. ② If **St Luke's-in-the-Fields** looks out of place, it is because it was built as a country church (1822). ③ Passers-by peer enviously at secluded **Grove Court** (1853), set back from a fine row of Federal houses, **Nos 4-10**, and two Greek Revival ones, **Nos 14-16**. ④ In **Commerce Street**, **Cherry Lane Theater** was founded in 1924 by the poet Edna St Vincent Millay and friends. **Nos 39-41** are an endearing pair of houses divided by a garden. The story that they were built by a sea captain for his warring daughters is, sadly, apocryphal. Opposite is family-run **Blue Mill Tavern** (**$**). ⑤ A mixture of tenements and houses, **Morton Street** still feels bohemian. Notice the ornate detailing on **No. 42** and the Federal doorway of **No. 59**. In **Bedford Street** you can't miss ⑥ **Twin Peaks**, a fantasy house created in 1925. Easy to miss is ⑦ **Chumley's** (**$**) as it has no sign, a hangover from its past as a prohibition speakeasy. The quick getaway passage is still there too. ⑧ Minute **No. 75½**, one window wide, was once the home of Edna St Vincent Millay. ⑨ The kids playing in bare, high-fenced **Walker Park** remind us that this is no quaint backwater but a pressurized inner city area, though ⑩ the lovely Italianate houses shaded by ginko trees overlooking it in **St Luke's Place** would have it otherwise. ⑪ Spacious, chic, *nouvelle* **Rakel** (**$$$**). ⑫ Laid-back **SOB's**, world music venue where tuxedos mingle with dreadlocks for a fun night out. ⑬ This stretch of **Bleeker Street** is steeped in venerable food shops, mostly Italian and heaven for foodies. Amongst them is **John's Pizzeria**, plain and perfect (**$**). ⑭ **Our Lady of Pompeii** (RC) where the local Italian community worship.

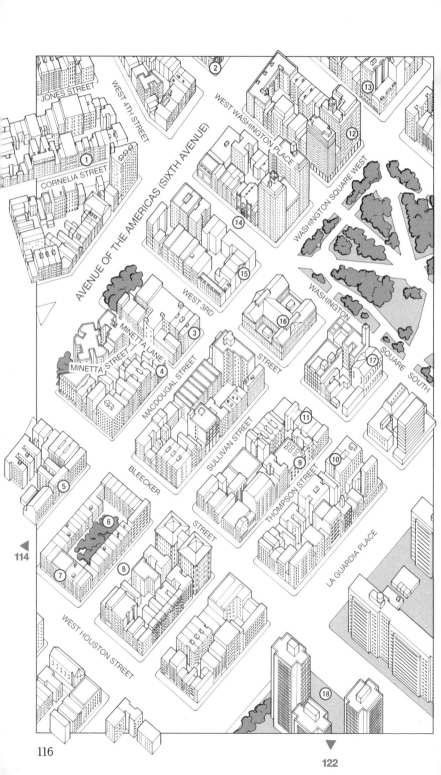

WEST 4TH STREET

②

WEST WASHINGTON PLACE

⑬

⑫

①

CORNELIA STREET

AVENUE OF THE AMERICAS (SIXTH AVENUE)

WASHINGTON SQUARE WEST

⑭

⑮

WEST 3RD

MINETTA LANE

③

WASHINGTON

MINETTA STREET

④

⑯

MACDOUGAL STREET

STREET

⑰

SQUARE SOUTH

⑤

SULLIVAN STREET

⑪

BLEECKER

⑨

⑩

THOMPSON STREET

⑥

◄
114

⑦

⑧

LA GUARDIA PLACE

WEST HOUSTON STREET

⑱

Greenwich Village/Macdougal Street

① Staying west of 6th Avenue (*see previous page*) **Sabor** (No. 20), cramped but convivial, serves Cuban food (**$$**), and **Lofti's** (No. 28) is fun for Moroccan cuisine (**$$**). ② **St Joseph's** (RC), decorous Greek Revival temple, with an interior like a glittering ballroom. Cross to Macdougal Street, where the bohemians came to life in cafés, bistros, attic studios and at the old Liberal Club (No. 137). The artistic impulse may have largely gone, but the area is still thronged with people late into the night and packed with dark little cabaret clubs and cafés. One of the oldest is ③ the delightfully gloomy **Caffè Reggio**. Notice opposite pretty **Nos 130/132**, the ironwork portico laced with wisteria. ④ **Minetta Tavern**, also little changed and full of memories (**$$**). ⑤ Florentine **Caffè Dante**. ⑥ These gaily painted mid-19thC houses designated the **Macdougal-Sullivan Historic District**, have an unusual communal garden, created in the l920s. ⑦ **Raffetto's** for pasta made on the premises since 1906. ⑧ **Sullivan Street Playhouse**, home of *The Fantasticks* for a record-breaking 30 years. ⑨ Pop into the scented **Bath House** for lovely lotions and potions. Opposite, ⑩ are an inviting clutch of restaurants, including **El Rincon de España** (**$$**) and **Grand Ticino** (**$$**). Next door is the quaint **Chess Shop**: play for an hourly fee or buy a hand-crafted chess set. Next to that – **Backgammon**.⑪ Ever-popular **Il Mulino** (86 W 3rd St; obscured; **$$$**); try at lunch. On the fringes of Washington Square (*see following page*), we find ⑫ the once-great, still-going **Coach House** (110 Waverly Pl.; obscured; **$$$**) and ⑬ opposite, basic **Washington Square** hotel (**$**). ⑭ West 4th Street includes the **United Methodist Church** of the Gay and Lesbian Community (gay New York had its roots in the Village), with the spooky-looking School of Sacred Arts next door. No. 131 is the star-studded **Blue Note Jazz Club**. Notice No. 136, completely criss-crossed by fire escapes. ⑮ Eugene O'Neill brought the **Provincetown Playhouse** here. Today it is home to the good old *Vampire Lesbians of Sodom*. Alongside are Federal houses **Nos 127-131**. No. 129 is the sweet **Lanterna di Vittorio** café. ⑯ Neo-Georgian **NYU School of Law Vanderbilt Hall** (1951). ⑰ Neo-Romanesque **Judson Memorial Baptist Church** complete with *campanile* (now student dormitories) and fine stained glass (McKim, Mead and White, 1892). ⑱ NYU-owned **Silver Towers**.

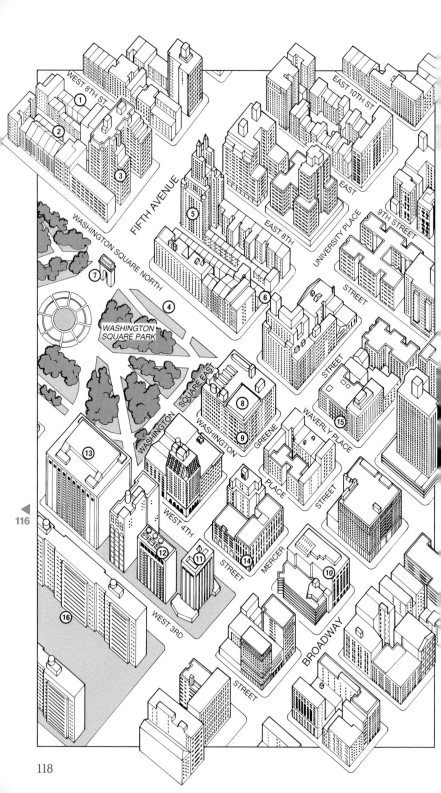

Greenwich Village/Washington Square

① **Eighth Street**, the Village's main commercial thoroughfare, is cluttered with fairly unmemorable stores, including lots selling clothing and shoes. ② **Macdougal Alley**, its picturesque houses converted from stables built in the 1850s, hides beneath the bulk of ③ apartment block **2 Fifth Avenue**. ④ A stroll along **Washington Square North** evokes a powerful sense of the past. Here are America's most beautiful Greek Revival town houses, built in the 1830s for Society, and later occupied by a horde of influential writers and artists, including of course Henry James, who based *Washington Square* on his grandmother's house, one of several which were torn down to make way for the extension to 2 Fifth Avenue. Notice the detailing on all the houses, the attractive wrought-iron balustrades and fences, and the fine pair of lions outside No. 6. West of Fifth Avenue, Nos 21-26 are intact. Of those on the east side, called 'The Row', Nos 7-13 are all artifice: only their façades remain, the interiors having been gutted to create an apartment house. ⑤ Restaurant **One Fifth** (obscured), kitted out with nautical nick-nacks salvaged from an ocean liner (**$$**). ⑥ Notice at the east end of cobbled **Washington Mews**, NYU's authentic-looking **Maison Française** and **Deutsches Haus**. ⑦ Stand in front of Stanford White's boldly majestic **Washington Arch** (1892) and gaze up Fifth Avenue, long and straight and fading into a blur of traffic and buildings. The arch stands in **Washington Square**, slightly wild Village playground and formerly a marsh, a mass burial ground and a site for public executions. The campus of **New York University** (NYU) occupies the east and south sides of the square. Buildings, marked out by huge purple flags, include ⑧ the **Main Building** (incorporating the innovative and elegant **Grey Art Gallery**); ⑨ **Brown Building**, notable for the tragic fire which once gutted it and cost 146 garment workers' lives (see plaque); ⑩ **Meyer Physics Hall**; ⑪ **Warren Weaver Hall**; ⑫ **Tisch Hall** and ⑬ the focal **Elmer Holmes Bobst Library** (Johnson and Foster, 1973). The stolid exterior, correctly faced in red brick, reveals a striking interior atrium. ⑭ **Bottom Line Cabaret**. ⑮ Flower-filled **Garvins**, with nightly piano music (**$$**). ⑯ These boring 1950s housing blocks go by the inappropriate name of **Washington Square Village**.

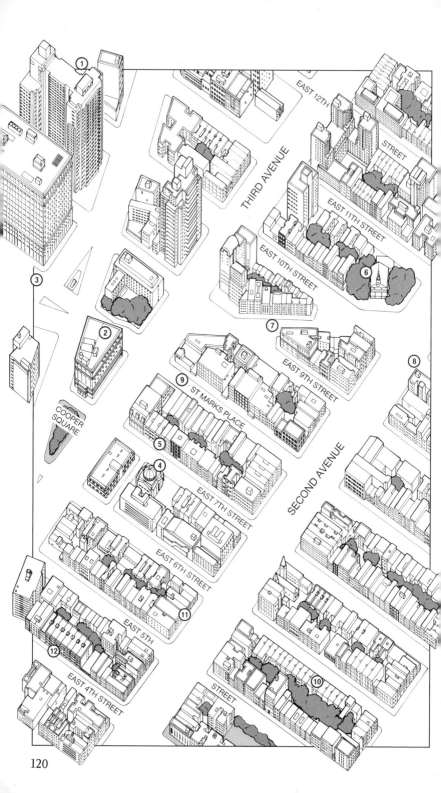

EAST 12TH

THIRD AVENUE

STREET

EAST 11TH STREET

EAST 10TH STREET

EAST 9TH STREET

ST MARKS PLACE

COOPER SQUARE

SECOND AVENUE

EAST 7TH STREET

EAST 6TH STREET

EAST 5TH

EAST 4TH STREET

STREET

East Village

Youth-orientated East Village, properly part of the harsh Lower East Side, gained its current identity in the 1960s when low rents attracted an overspill from its bohemian neighbor, Greenwich Village (*see pages 115-19*). Flea markets, cafés, dance spots, theaters, strange little shops that come and go, a sprinkling of historic landmarks and a rich ethnic mix create the scene. ① On a bend in Broadway at E 10th Street, **Grace Church** (obscured) is a lovely sight. It was built in Gothic Revival style by James Renwick (then aged 23) in 1846. ② Peter Cooper, self-made industrial millionaire and philanthropist, founded **Cooper Union** in 1859. This portentious brownstone building was the first college of further education which was (and still is) free and open to anyone, regardless of sex, wealth, creed or colour. ③ In 1849 **Astor Place** saw a bloody riot, with many deaths, caused by rival supporters of two actors, Edwin Forrest and William Macready, which blew up while Englishman Macready was trying to get through Macbeth inside the long-gone Astor Place Opera House. Look out for the **barber's shop** at No. 2 where you can line up for a cut or a '50s quiff. ④ **St George's Ukranian Catholic Church** is the focal point of a close-knit Ukranian community centered on this street. Opposite, ⑤ is **Surma** (No. 11), a colorful, long-established Ukranian emporium selling books, music, embroidered clothes, icons, *kilims* and their famous painted eggs. At No. 15 is **McSorley's Old Ale House**, the city's oldest saloon (1854). ⑥ A Georgian country church when it was built in 1799, **St Mark's-in-the-Bowery** stands on the site of Governor Peter Stuyvesant's private chapel. Almost destroyed by fire in 1978 but now restored, this in an active center of community arts. ⑦ **Stuyvesant Street** breaks the grid pattern by following the driveway to the Governor's mansion. The gracious Anglo-Italianate houses here and in E 10th Street form the **Renwick Triangle** (James Renwick, 1861). Note No. 21, the early Federal **Stuyvesant-Fish House**. ⑧ East Side institution, **Second Avenue Deli ($)**. ⑨ **St Mark's Place**, gritty, disturbing, raucous center of downtown youth culture. ⑩ **Little India**: take your pick from a block jammed with Indian restaurants. ⑪ At **No. 91**, in 1910, a piano was hauled up to the Gershwin family apartment and set 12 year-old George on course for fame. ⑫ **Cucina di Pesce** (No. 87): bargain prices, long lines and great fish and pasta dishes ($).

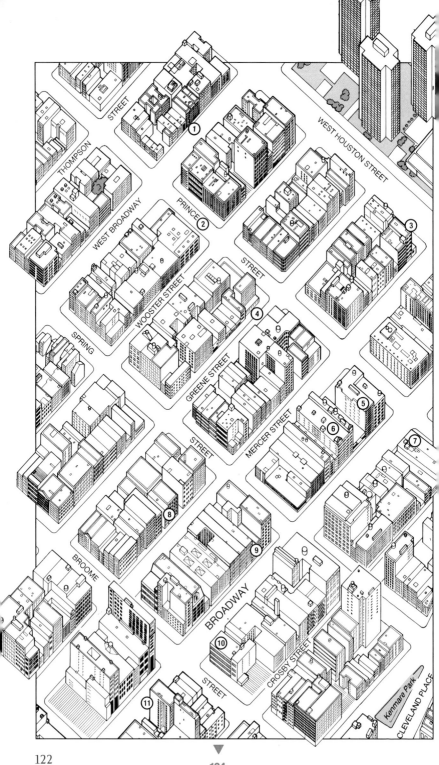

THOMPSON STREET

WEST HOUSTON STREET

WEST BROADWAY

PRINCE STREET

WOOSTER STREET

STREET

SPRING

GREENE STREET

MERCER STREET

STREET

BROOME

STREET

BROADWAY

CROSBY STREET

STREET

Kenmare Park

CLEVELAND PLACE

1
2
3
4
5
6
7
8
9
10
11

SoHo

Named for its location, south of Houston Street, SoHo is famous for its 19thC Renaissance cast-iron buildings, distinctively criss-crossed with fire escapes. Most were built as warehouses, but now provide studio space for the artists who began to flock here in the 1960s. ① **West Broadway**, typical mix of esoteric stores, galleries and restaurants: **Rizzoli** art bookstore (No. 454) looks stunning after a facelift; exotic jewelry at **Sally Hawkins Gallery** (No. 448); hip Sicilian restaurant, Vucciria, at No. 422 (**$$$**); **Ad Hoc Softwares**, full of lovely things for the home (No. 410); cluster of galleries in **SoHotel** (No. 382). ② An array of food stores and restaurants tempt the palate in **Prince Street: Raoul's Boucherie and Charcuterie** (No. 179) for home-made sausages; **Vesuvio's** real Italian bakery (No. 160); **Dean and Deluca Coffee and Tea** (No. 121) for a Danish and espresso in a loft. Spot the difference between the true facade of **Nos 112-114** and Richard Haas' brilliant *trompe l'oeil* round the corner. ③ Avant-garde **New Museum of Contemporary Art**. ④ Charming cobbled **Greene Street**, heart of SoHo Cast-Iron Historic District; outstanding are **Nos 28-30** and **72-76** by Isaac F. Duckworth. Restaurants jostle for space with galleries and specialty shops: among them, **Greene Street Restaurant** (No. 101), good food and jazz (**$$**); **5 & 10 No Exaggeration**, unique '40s-style restaurant in an antique shop (**$$$**); **Rosa Esman** (No. 70) for modern art; **Back Pages Antiques** (No. 125) for Wurlitzers, barbers' poles and other '50s memorabilia. ⑤ Ernest Flagg's novel **Little Singer Building** (1904), in cast-iron with terracotta relief panels. ⑥ Vast gray granite and cast-iron **Rouss Building** (1889). ⑦ No ordinary grocery, **Dean and DeLuca** is an imposing white pillared space, where mouthwatering delicacies – ravioli stuffed with truffles, scallop mousse, sun-dried tomatoes, exotic teas and herbs – are enticingly displayed, together with a formidable battery of cookware. Galleries occupy the floors above. ⑧ **Enchanted Forest**, toystore with a woodland setting. ⑨ All that remains of the former sumptuous **St Nicholas Hotel** (1854). ⑩ 'Parthenon of Cast-Iron Architecture', the **Haughwout Building** was in fact modeled on a Venetian *palazzo*. James P. Gaynor designed it to house Eder V. Haughwout's glass, china and silverware emporium and America's first steam-powered passenger elevator. ⑪ Titanic in scale, but delicate in its filigree detailing, Richard Morris Hunt's **Roosevelt Building** (1874).

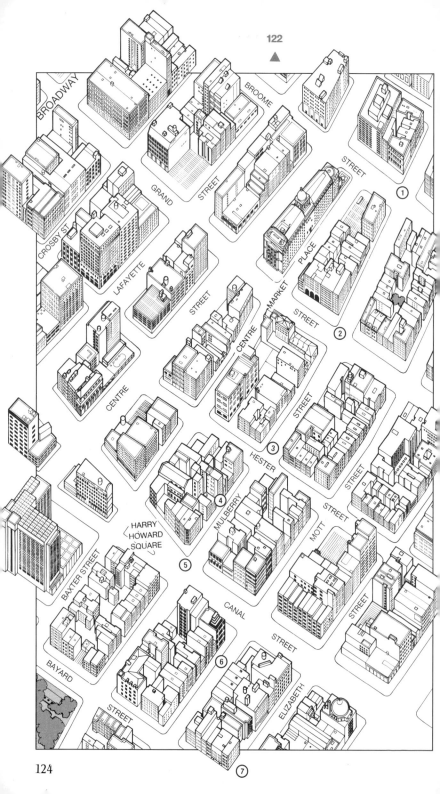

Little Italy and Chinatown

Though still a focus for the now-dispersed Italian community, and redolent of *la patria*, (especially in Sept, during the *Festa di San Gennaro*), Little Italy has shrunk to no more than a short stretch of **Mulberry Street**. ① At this intersection we find jolly **Grotta Azzura** (**$$**) and **Caffè Roma** (**$**), quite unchanged. ② Mulberry and Grand mark the district's center. Here are ravioli companies, Italian importers, **Rossi**, a Little Italy gift shop, **Ferrara**, touristy but justifiably famous for its pastries, the austere Società San Gennaro, and once-favorite **Angelo's** (**$$**). Also **Taormina** (**$$**), which stands out amongst the mainly mediocre trattorias of Little Italy. ③ **Umberto's Clam House** (**$**), where Joey Gallo was 'blown away', is a landmark at Mulberry and Hester. **Ceramica** sells irresistible Italian ceramics and pottery. ④ Toward Canal Street you will pass popular **Il Cortile** (**$$**), **Esposito Meats**, and set back, the blocklike **Church of the Most Precious Blood**. ⑤ **Canal Street** marks the boundary with Chinatown which is thriving and growing, even threading north through streets that were once strictly Italian. Everything is Chinese, from banks to funeral parlors, the dismal streets enlivened by pagoda roofs, Buddhist temples and street stalls. The tiny area was first appropriated in the mid-19thC by male workers intent on making money and going home. Instead they stayed to make this the most enclosed and authentic Chinese community in the West, with a population of around 125,000. Stroll the streets, principally ⑥ **Mott**, ⑦ **Bayard** and **Pell** (off map) and try to catch Chinese New Year (first full moon after Jan 19). Look out for: **Kam Man Food Products** (200 Canal St, between Mott and Mulberry), and southwards along Mott St: **Eastern States Buddhist Temple** (No. 646); **Lung Fong Bakery** – try the winter melon cake (No. 41); **Quong Xuen Shing** for porcelain goods (No. 32); **Tak Sung Tung**, herbalist where you can stock up on deer's tail extract (No. 11); and **Chinatown Fair**, a video game arcade where you can play tick-tack-toe with a chicken. Amongst the hordes of cheap, scruffy, reliable restaurants, **Mandarin Court**, 61 Mott St, (**$$**), and **HSF**, 116 Bowery (**$**), are good for *dim sum*. **Oriental Town** (14 Elizabeth St) for seafood (**$**); **Peking Duck House** (22 Mott St; **$**) for great Peking Duck; and **20 Mott Street** for excellent Cantonese food (**$**).

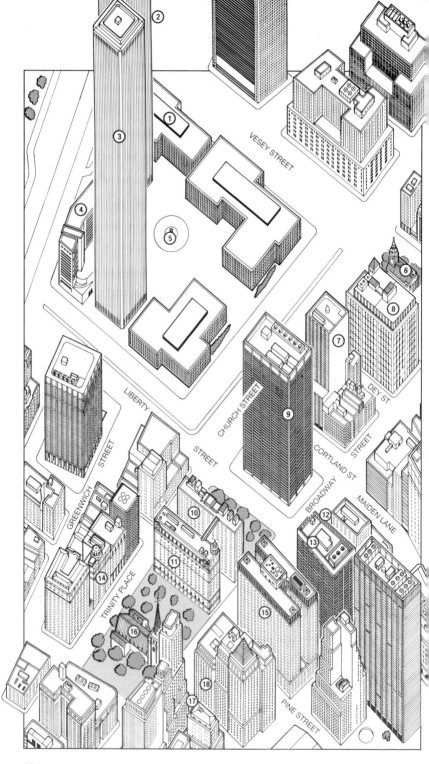

VESEY STREET

LIBERTY

STREET

CHURCH STREET

CORTLAND ST

DEY ST

BROADWAY

MAIDEN LANE

GREENWICH

STREET

STREET

TRINITY PLACE

PINE STREET

126

World Trade Center

Heart of ① the world's largest commercial complex, the **World Trade Center**, the 1,350 foot, 110-story **Twin Towers** look most impressive from a distance: two slender shafts of steel that tower over their neighbors and glisten in the sun. ② In **WTC 1**, there is a spectacular view of the city from the famous **Windows on the World** restaurant on the 107th floor (**$$$**). ③ The panorama is equally breathtaking from **WTC 2**'s enclosed **Observation Deck** and open **rooftop promenade**. Look down on ant-sized people, scurrying from dinky cars to toy-town offices. ④ **Vista International Hotel**, agreeable Hilton overlooking the Hudson River (**$$$**). ⑤ Dominating the 5-acre plaza, Fritz Koenig's dramatic **Globe sculpture**. ⑥ New York's only surviving pre-revolutionary building, Thomas McBean's lovely Georgian **St Paul's Chapel**. ⑦ Splendid steel eagles guard the entrances of model Art Deco **East River Savings Bank**. ⑧ The original **American Telephone and Telegraph Company** (1915-22), an eccentric classical building with more columns than the Parthenon. ⑨ **One Liberty Plaza**, 1974 steel monolith. ⑩ **U.S. Realty Building** and ⑪ **Trinity Building**, a pair of pleasing Gothic-style skyscrapers. ⑫ Former **New York State Chamber of Commerce** (65 Liberty St; obscured), an imposing Beaux Arts building. ⑬ Glass panels are divided by black spandrels in Skidmore, Owings and Merrill's glossy 1960s skyscraper, **Marine Midland Bank Building**. ⑭ The crenellated dome atop **74 Trinity Place** is a secret purpose-built vestry for Trinity Church, done out in medieval style, complete with misericords. ⑮ The outcry caused by Ernest Graham's 1915 **Equitable Building**, 1.2 million square feet of office space built on less than 1 acre, resulted in the 1916 zoning law. The seafood is all deliciously fresh at no-frills fish restaurant, **Vincent Petrosini** (100 Greenwich St; off map), but, if they're in season, the soft shell crabs are a must (**$**). ⑯ The 'black widow of Broadway', **Trinity Church** is having her face washed and changing back to brownstone. The third church on this site, it was built in 1846 by Richard Upjohn, and boasts three sets of massive bronze doors by Richard Morris Hunt. In ⑰ **Wall Street**, the world's most famous banking street, ⑱ **Bank of Tokyo** (Bruce Price, 1895) has been sympathetically modernized, retaining J. Massey Rhind's classical statues, perched above a colonnade.

South Street Seaport

① An eye-catching prank, painted in glorious pastels, the cast-iron **Bennett Building** (1872). ② Philip Johnson and John Burgee's controversial post-modern office building, **33 Maiden Lane**, complete with turrets and battlements. ③ Top security **Federal Reserve Bank of New York**, mock Renaissance *palazzo*, where hoards of gold are stored in five underground stories. ④ Still sporting its original sign, but now a co-op, the Romanesque Revival **Excelsior Power Company Building** (1888). ⑤ An amusing neon-lit tube forms the entrance to New York's 'fun skyscraper', **127 John Street** (1969). ⑥ **Titanic Memorial Lighthouse**, moved here from the Seamen's Church Institute above East River, marks the entrance to **South Street Seaport**, 19thC shipping capital of the New World, massively restored by the Rouse Company. The result is a seductive, but over-commercialized area: a play place, where tourists mingle with Wall Street workers. ⑦ During the excavation for Fox and Fowle's dramatic post-modern highrise, HQ of the **National Westminster Bank**, the hull of an 18thC British merchant ship was discovered. ⑧ **New 'Bogardus' Building**, replica of the city's oldest cast-iron building, Edgar Laing Store, built by Bogardus on the corner of Murray and Washington Streets in 1848. **Fulton Market** (11 Fulton St; off map), 1983 reconstruction of an 1882 covered market. ⑨ Focus of the Seaport, **Schermerhorn Row** was a cluster of early 19thC warehouses, built by speculator Peter Schermerhorn. Still charming despite heavy restoration, it now includes several pricey stores, two seafood restaurants, **Sloppy Louie's ($$$)** and **Sweets ($$$)**, a pub, **North Star**, and **South Street Seaport Museum**. ⑩ Art Nouveau gem, the old **Maximilian Morgenthau tobacco warehouse**. ⑪ **Fulton Fish Market** is a genuine relic of the past. A cavernous old tin building, with huge long tables and vast weighing scales, it is a hive of activity between midnight and 8am. Early birds can take a guided tour at 6am from April to October and sample the catch of the day for breakfast. ⑫ **Pier 17** boasts three stories, bursting with cafés, shops and stalls, and a great view of the harbor. Reminders of the Seaport's maritime past are the tall ships, ⑬ **Peking**, a magnificent four-masted bark (1911), and ⑭ the three-masted English square-rigger **Wavertree** (1885).

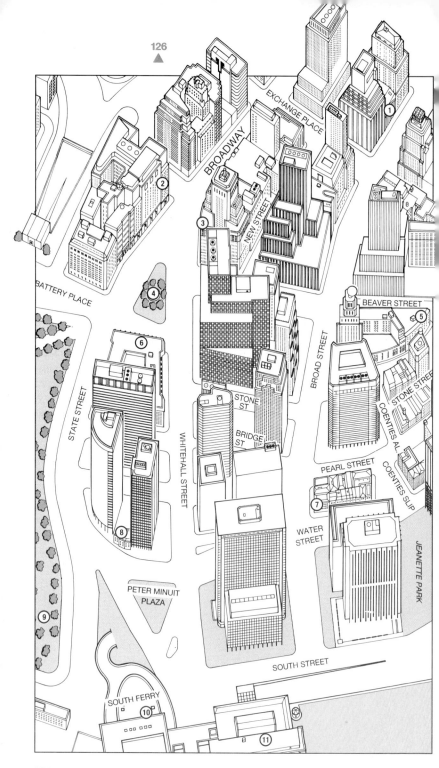

126 ▲

Battery Park

The twisting streets, typical of Manhattan's southern tip and in contrast to the uptown grid pattern, are a reminder that this is the oldest part of the city, the settlers' *Nieuwe Amsterdam*. ① A buttonwood tree outside George B. Post's impressive classical **New York Stock Exchange** serves as a memorial to the merchants who met daily under such a tree and in 1792 drew up a trading agreement (**Gallery** open to the public). ② Passengers on the Queen Mary would have booked their tickets in the wonderful vaulted Great Hall of the old **Cunard Building**, also noteworthy for its 1920s Renaissance façade. Opposite is the bowed front of ③ the former **Standard Oil Building**, from where John D. Rockefeller ran his empire. ④ The city's first park, **Bowling Green**, was a parade ground, rented in 1733 by citizens who paid the princely sum of one peppercorn a year. The park's railings survive, but in 1776 after the reading of the Declaration of Independence, patriots destroyed the crowns that topped them and a statue of George III that stood here. ⑤ As much an institution as the New York Stock Exchange, **Delmonico's** occupies a grand 19thC building and specializes in simply cooked meat and fish (**$$**). In tranquil **Hanover Square** (off map), watched over by the figure of Dutch goldsmith, **Abraham de Peyster**, is the attractive Anglo-Italianate **India House** (1851-4). ⑥ On the site of the settlers' Fort Amsterdam, the former **United States Custom House** (Cass Gilbert, 1907) is the apogee of the Beaux Arts style, a mansion in dark gray granite, with four white limestone monuments by Daniel Chester French, symbolizing the continents and providing an inspired contrast. No less magnificent is the **oval rotunda** inside, with murals by Reginald Marsh. ⑦ **Fraunces Tavern**, re-creation of an inn on this site where Washington bade farewell to his troops on 4th December 1783; it now includes a **restaurant** and **museum**. ⑧ Lovely Federal **Watson House**, now the **Chapel of our Lady of the Rosary** and **Shrine of Saint Elizabeth Anne Seton**, America's first saint. ⑨ An oasis of lawns and trees, **Battery Park** took its name from the battery of cannon that stood here in the 1680s. From the water's edge (off map), there is a fine view of the **Statue of Liberty** and **Ellis Island**. Among Battery Park's many monuments, seek out the early 19thC defense post, **Castle Clinton** (off map). ⑩ 1950s **Staten Island Ferry Terminal** and the brand-new **South Ferry Plaza**. ⑪ Crumbling Beaux Arts **Battery Maritime Building**, made of sheet metal and painted green to resemble copper.

GENERAL POINTS OF INTEREST

A

American Academy of Dramatic Arts 109
American Bible Society 33
American Women's Association 37

B

banks
   Bowery Savings 93
   Chase Manhattan 41
   Chemical 75, 81
   Crossland Savings 87
   East River Savings 127
   Federal Reserve Bank of New York 129
   Israel Discount 81
bars *see* pubs and bars
Bird Sanctuary 50
Bronx, The 43
buildings, including apartments and
  houses
   1 Park Avenue 111
   2 Fifth Avenue 119
   2 Park Avenue 109
   32 West 40th Street 89
   33 Maiden Lane 129
   36 West 35th Street 97
   57 Park Avenue 101
   74 Trinity Place 127
   101 Park Avenue 93
   127 John Street 129
   270 Park Avenue 73
   274 Madison Avenue 91
   425 Lexington Avenue 93
   500 Park Avenue Tower 55, 65
   575 Fifth Avenue 73
   750 Seventh Avenue 45
   780 Third Avenue 75
   1675 Broadway 45
   A&S Plaza 87
   AT&T Building 53
   Alwyn Court 39
   American Standard Building 89
   American Telephone and Telegraph Company
     Building 127
   American Tower 59
   Amro Bank Building 55
   Ansonia Apartments 35
   Appellate Division, New York State Supreme
     Court Building 107
   Apthorp Apartments 35
   Aramo Building 55
   Associated Press Building 61
   Bank of Tokyo Building 127
   Bankers Trust Building 73
   Battery Maritime Building 131
   Bennett Building 129
   Bowery Savings Bank Building 93
   Bowker Building 109
   British Empire Building 61
   Brown Building, New York University 119
   Bryant Park Studios 89
   Burden House 29
   Bush Tower 69

   CBS Building 49
   Celanese Building 59
   Chanin Building 93
   Channel Gardens 61
   Chemcourt 75
   Chrysler Building 93
   Citicorp Center 67
   Conference Building, United Nations 105
   Cunard Building 131
   Daily News Building 103
   Dakota, The 35
   Daytop Village 89
   Dehamar Mansion 99
   Deutsches Haus, New York University 119
   E. F. Hutton Building 49
   Emmet Building 109
   Empire State Building 97
   Equitable Building 127
   Equitable Center 45
   Excelsior Power Company Building 129
   Exxon Building 45
   Factory, The 109
   Ford Foundation Building 95, 103
   Fred F. French Building 81
   Fuller Building 55
   GE Building 75
   General Assembly Building, United Nations 105
   General Motors Building 53
   Gilsey House 107
   Goelet Building 61
   Grace Building 51
   H. Percy Silver Parish House 99
   Hammond House 29
   Harkness House 31
   Haughwout Building 123
   Health Education Centre Building 111
   Hearst Magazine Building 37
   Helmsley Building 83
   Herald Center 87
   Heron Tower 65
   Hoffman Hall, General Theological Seminary 113
   Hôtel des Artistes 35
   India House 41, 131
   International House 61
   J. Hampton Robb Mansion 111
   J. P. Morgan Jr House 99
   J. P. Stevens Tower 59
   James F. D. Lanier Residence 111
   Kaskel and Kaskel Building 97
   Knox Hat Building 89
   Lever House 65
   Lincoln Building 81
   Lincoln Plaza Tower 33
   Lipstick Building 67
   Little Singer Building 123
   MONY Tower 47
   McGraw-Hill Building 59
   Madison Avenue Baptist Church Parish House 109
   Maison Franaise, New York University 119
   Main Building, New York University 119
   Marine Midland Bank Building 127
   Maximilian Morgenthau Tobacco Warehouse
     Building 129
   Metropolitan Life Insurance Company Building
     107

Meyer Physics Hall, New York University 119
Midtown North Precinct 37
Milton Glaser Design Studio 111
Mobil Building 93
Morgan Bank Headquarters 45
Museum Twoer 49
National Maritime Union Building 113
National Westminster Bank Building 129
Nelson Tower 87
New 'Bogardus' Building 129
New York Life Building 107
New York State Chamber of Commerce Building 127
New York Stock Exchange Building 131
New York Telephone Building 69
One Astor Plaza 57
One Central Park Place 37
One Liberty Plaza 127
One Penn Plaza 85
One Times Square 69
Osborne's 39
Palazzo d'Italia 61
Pan Am Building 81, 83
Paramount Building 57
Park Avenue Plaza 75
Park Vendôme Apartments 37
Petrola House 63
Philip Morris Building 81
Phoenix Building 71
Plaza, The 53
Port of New York Authority Commerce Building 113
RCA (now GE *qv*) building 45, 61
Raymond R. Corbett Building 109
Remsen Building 109
Republic National Bank Tower 89
Rockefeller Apartments 63
Roosevelt Building 123
Rouss Building 123
Seagram Buildinig 65
Secretariat Building, United Nations 105
Silver Towers, New York University 117
Sloane House YMCA 85
Solow Building 51, 79
South Ferry Plaza 131
Standard Oil Building 131
Staten Island Ferry Termingal 131
Stuyvesant-Fish House 121
Swissôtel Drake 65
Time & Life Building 45
Tisch Hall, New York University 119
Tishman Building 49
Trump Tower 53
Tudor City 103
Trinity Building 127
Twin Peaks 115
Twin Towers, World Trade Center 127
United Nations Buildings 103, 105
United Nations Plaza 105
United States Custom House 131
United States Realty Building 127
Universal Pictures Building 65
Vanderbilt Hall, New York University School of Law 117
Villard House 63
W. R. Grace Building 79
Warren House Hall, New York University 119
Washington Square Village 119
Watson House 131
West Building, General Theological Seminary 113
World Wide Plaza 43

C

cafés and restaurants
Adrienne 63
Ambassador's Grill 105
An American Place 109
Angelo's 125
Aquavit 63
Arcadia 41
Audrome 57
Aureole 55
Aurora 73
B. Smith's 57
Back Porch 111
Bangkok Cuisine 45
Barbetta 57
Bellini by Cipriani 45
Bottom Line Cabaret 119
Brasserie, The 65
Broadway Diner 47
C. I. Ristorante 93
Cabana Carioca 59
Café de la Paix 51
Café Un Deux Trois 49
Café des Artistes 35
Caffé Cielo 37
Caffé Dante 117
Caffé Reggio 117
Caffé Roma 125
Cajun 113
Caramba 47
Carolina 57
Cedars of Lebanon 109
Chalet Suisse 73
Chelsea Place 113
Chez Napoleon 43
Christine's 101
Chumley's 115
Coach House 117
Corrado 49
Courtyard Caf 101
Cucina di Pesce 121
Da Tommaso 37
Darbar 51
Dean and Deluca Coffee and Tea 123
Delegates Dining Room, United Nations 105
Dlices de France 91
Delmonico's 131
Dock's Oyster Bar 103
Dolci on the Park 99
El Rincon de España 117
Four Seasons, The 65
Gallagher's 45
Garvins 119
Ginger Man 35
Gran Caff Bitici 67
Grand Ticino 117

Grand Tier 33
Grappino 89
Greene Street Restaurant 123
Grotta Azura 125
HSF 125
Hard Rock Caf 39
Harry's Bar 45
Hatsuhana 73
Horn and Hardat automat 103
Il Cortile 125
Il Mulino 117
Il Nido 67
India Pavilion 47
Jerusalem 77
Jockey Club, The 51
Joe Allen 57
John's Pizzeria 115
Keen's Steak and Chop House 97
La Côte Basque 53
La Grenouille 63
La Resrve 61
Lafayette 65
Lanterna di Vittoria 117
Lattanzi 57
Le Bernardin 45
Le Cygne 65
Le Relais 41
Le Riva 57
Les Pleiades 31
Les Pyréneés, Tout Va Bien 43
Lofti's 117
Lutéce 67
Maison Japonaise 101
Man Ray 113
Mandarin Court 125
Manhattan Ocean Club 51
Marchi's 111
Miss Ruby's Café 113
Mitsukoshi 55, 65
Nanni 95
Nippon 67
No Exaggeration 123
Oak Room, The 71
One Fifth 119
Oriental Town 125
Orso 57
Oyster Bar 51, 93
Palm 95
Palms Too 95
Park Bistro 109
Pasta Prego 71
Peking Duck House 125
Pen and Pencil 95
Petrossian 39
Pisces 65
Porteroz 101
Prunelle 53
Quilted Giraffe 53
Raffetto's 117
Rainbow Room Restaurant 61
Rakel 115
Regina's 55
Rene Pujol 43
Restaurant Raphael 63

Rumpelmayer's 51
Russian Tea Room 39
SOB's 115
Sabor 117
Salta in Bocca 109
Sardi's 57
Sfuzzi 35
Shun Lee Palace 67
Siam Inn 47
Sloppy Louie's 129
Sonia Rose 109
Sparks 95
Sunny East 89
Sweets 129˙
Symphony Caf 47
T.S. Ma 85
Taormina 125
Tavern on the Green 35
Time and Again 101
Toscana 67
Trader Vic's 51
Trattoria Dell'Arte 39
Trixie's 57
Umberto's Clam House 125
View, The 57
Vincent Petrosini 127
Vucciria 123
Windows on the World, World Trade Center 127
Woods 37th 77
Zarela 67
Castle Clinton 131
Chinatown 125
churches, synagogues and temples
    Armenian Evangelical Church 111
    Central Synagogue 65
    Chapel of our Lady of the Rosary 131
    Chapel of the Good Shepherd, General
        Theological Seminary 113
    Christ Church (Methodist) 55
    Church of Christ Scientist 81
    Church of St Saviour 101
    Church of the Covenant 103
    Church of the Heavenly Rest 29
    Church of the Most Precious Blood 125
    Church of the Transfiguration 107
    Episcopal Church of the Incarnation 99
    Eastern States Buddhist Temple 125
    Fifth Avenue Presbyterian Church 51
    Fifth Avenue Synagogue 41
    First Moravian Church 109
    Grace Church 121
    Holy Trinity Lutheran Church 35
    Judson Memorial Baptist Church 117
    Marble Collegiate Church 107
    Mecca Temple 49
    New Church (Swedenborgian) 111
    Our Lady of Pompeii (RC) Church 115
    St Agnes Church 95
    St Bartholomew's Church 75
    St Benedict Church 43
    St Benedict's Church 37
    St George Tropoforos Hellenic Orthodox Church
        37
    St George's Ukrainian Catholic Church 121

St John's (RC) Church 85
St Joseph's (RC) Church, Greenwich 117
St Luke's-in-the-Fields Church, Greenwich 115
St Mark's-in-the-Bowery 121
St Mary-the-Virgin (RC) Church 59
St Patrick's Cathedral 63
St Paul's Chapel 127
St Peter's Church, Chelsea 113
St Peter's Lutheran Church 67
St Stephen's Church 109
St Thomas' Church 49
Temple Emanu-El 41
Trinity Church, Broadway 113, 127
United Methodist Church 117
Christie's 55
cinemas
    New Amsterdam 57
City Center of Music and Drama 49
Clinton 43
clubs
    21 Club 49
    Art Students League 39
    Blue Note Jazz Club 117
    Century Club 79
    Collector's Club 99
    Colony Club 109
    Engineers' Club 89
    Grolier Club 55, 109
    Harvard Club 71, 79
    Liberal Club 117
    Lotos Club 41
    Metropolitan Club 41
    New York Road Runners Club 29
    New York Yacht Club 71, 79
    Racquet and Tennis Club 75
    Republican Club 89
    Union Club 99
    Union League Club 31, 41, 99
    University Club 63
    Yale Club 81
concert halls
    Alice Tully Hall 33
    Avery Fisher Hall 33
    Carnegie Hall 39
    Graduate Center, New York University 79
    Guggenheim Band Shell 33
    Juillard Recital Hall 33
    Metropolitan Opera House 33
    Radio City Music Hall 61
Convention and Visitors Bureau (New York) 39

E

East River 103, 105
Ellis Island 131

F

Fur District 85

G

galleries
    Grey Art Gallery, New York University 119
    Pace Gallery 65
    Wally Findlay Gallery 53
    Wildenstein 41

Garment Center 77, 89
General Post Office 85
Greenwich Village 45, 114-19
Guiness World Exhibit Hall 97

H

hotels
    Algonquin 71, 79
    Astor 43
    Bedford 101
    Beerly 75
    Carlyle 31
    Crown Plaza 43
    Chatwal Inn 103
    Doral Court 101
    Doral Park Avenue 91
    Doral Tuscany 101
    Edison 43
    Eichner 59
    Elyse 65
    Empire 33
    Grand Bay 45
    Halloran House 75
    Helmsley Palace 63
    Hotel Clinton 97
    Hotel Dorset 49
    Hotel Lowell 41
    Hotel Martinique 97
    Hotel Pierre 41
    Hotel Salisbury 39
    Hotel Wellington 49
    Inter-Continental 75
    Kitano 99
    Knickerbocker 43, 69
    Loews Summit 75
    Mark, The 31
    Marriott Marquis 57
    Mayflower 35
    Milford Plaza 57
    Morgan's 99
    New York Helmsley 103
    New York Hilton 49
    New York Penta 85
    Omni Park Central 47
    Paramount 43
    Parker Meridien 39
    Peninsula 63
    Plaza 51
    Regent of New York 55
    Ritz-Carlton 51
    Roger Smith Winthrop 95
    Roosevelt 83
    Royalton 43, 79, 99
    St Moritz 51
    Sharaton Centre 47
    Sheraton Park Avenue 101
    Surrey Suite 31
    United Nations Plaza 105
    Vista International 127
    Waldorf-Astoria 75
    Washington Square 117
    Wentworth 71
    Wyndham 51
Hudson River

I

institutions
General Society of Mechanics and Tradesmen 79
Guggenheim Institute 29
Kosciuszko Foundation 41
Lincoln Center for the Performing Arts 33
National Academy of Design 29
Smithsonian Institute 29
Ukrainian Institute of America 31
Yivo Institute for Jewish Research 29
J. G. Jung Center 91
Jacob Javits Convention Center 85

L

libraries
Donnell Library Center 49
Elmer Holmes Bobst Library, New York University 119
Hammerskjold Library, United Nations Headquarters 105
Library and Museum of the Performing Arts 33
Morgan Library 99
New York Public Library 49
Pierpont Morgan Library 99
St Mark's Library, General Theological Seminary 113
Lincoln Center
Little India 121

C

Macdonald-Sullivan Historic District 117
Madison Square Garden Center 85
Murray Farm 99
museums
American Craft 49
American Folk Art 35
American Museum of National History 35
Cooper-Hewitt 29
Fraunces Tavern 131
Frick Collection 31
Library and Museum of the Performing Arts 33
Metropolitan Museum of Art 31
Modern Art 49
TV and Radio 49
New Museum of Contemporary Art 123
South Street Seaport 129
Whitney Museum of American Art 31, 45, 81

N

NBC Studios 61
New York City Ballet and Opera Companies 33
New York School of Applied Design for Women 109
New York Society for Ethical Culture 35
New York State Supreme Court 107
New York University 79, 117, 119
newspapers and magazines
Life magazine 97
New York Herald 87
New York Times 57, 69
New York Tribune 87
New Yorker, The 71

O

opera houses
Astor Place Opera House (former) 121
Metropolitan Opera 51

P

parks
Battery Park 131
Bowling Green 131
Bryant Park 68, 78-9, 88, 89
Central Park 31, 34, 38, 39, 40, 50, 53
Damrosch Park 33
Greenwich Park 67
Madison Square Garden 43, 84-5, 107
Madison Square Park 106, 107
Paley Park 53
Turtle Bay Gardens 105
Tudor City parks 95
Walker Park 114, 115
Washington Square Park 116, 118
Polish Consulate 99
public houses and wine bars
Blue Bar 71
Blue Mill Tavern 115
Fraunces Tavern 131
McSorley's Old Ale House 121
Michael's Pub 67
Minetta Tavern 117
North Star 129
O'Neal's 33
P. J. Clark's 67
Public Library 79, 89

R

Renwick Triangle 121
Roseland Dance Hall 45
Rockefeller Center 45, 59, 69

S

San Juan Hill 37
School of Law, New York University 117 schools and colleges
Convent of the Sacred Heart 29
Cooper Union 121
General Theological Seminary 113
Juillard School of Music 33
Lycée Français 31
St David's 29
sculptures and statues
Abraham de Peyster (statue) 131
Columbus 39
Globe 127
horsemen 111
Maine Memorial 39
monument and murals at United States Custom House 131
Obelisk to Peace 111
Performance Machine 83
Pullitzer Fountain 53
Sculpture Garden 49
General Sherman (statue) 53
Statue of Liberty 35, 131
Shepherds 65
Seth Thomas clock 79

Washington Arch 119
ships
 Peking 129
 Wavertree 129
shops and stores
 Abraham and Straus 87
 Ad Hoc Softwares 123
 American Radiator Co 89
 Ann Taylor 53
 Antonovich 85
 Argosy 55
 Art-Max 77
 Baccarat 55
 Back Pages Antiques 123
 Backgammon 117
 Ballet Shop, The 33
 Banana Republic 55
 Bath House 117
 Bergdorf Goodman 51, 53
 Birger Christensen 85
 Brentano's 73
 Bridge Kitchenware 67
 Brooks Brothers 81
 Buccellati 55
 Bulgari 51
 Burberry's 53
 Carnegie Deli 47
 Cartier 63
 Caswell-Massey 75
 Ceramica 125
 Chanel 53
 Charivari '57' 51
 Chess Shop 117
 Chinatown Fair 125
 Churchill's 41
 Coach Store, The 41
 Cole-Haan 55
 Coliseum Books 47
 Complete Traveller 99
 Crabtree and Evelyn 61
 Crouch and Fitzgerald 73
 Dean and Deluca 123
 Drama Bookshop 59
 E. Braun 41
 Elizabeth Arden 53
 Enchanted Forest 123
 Esposito Meats 125
 F. A. O. Schwarz 53
 F. R. Tripler 81
 Fellman 81
 Ferragamo 51
 Ferrara 125
 Fortunoff 53
 Fraser Morris 31
 Fulton Fish Market 129
 Fulton Market 129
 Gimbel's 87
 Godiva Chocolatier 53
 Goldberg's Marine Distributors 89
 Golden-Feldman 85
 Gordon Button Co 77
 Gorham's 97
 Gotham Book Mart and Gallery 61
 Gucci 53

Guy Laroche 55
Hammacher Schlemmer 55
Harry Winston 51
Helene Arpels 55
Henry Westpfal 97
Herms 53
Hotalings 69
Hyman Hendler 77
I. Miller 59
J. J. Applebaum's 85
J. P. French Bakery 63
Jaeger 53, 61
Kam Man Food Products 125
Kaplan's 61
Kaufman 75
La Maison Franaise 61
Lalique 41
Laura Ashley 41, 53
Lederer 55
Li-Lac 115
Limited, The 41
Lloyd and Haig 91
Lord and Taylor 89
Louis Vuitton 55
Lung Fong Bakery 125
M&J Trimmings Co 77
M. J. Knoud Saddlery 41
McNulty's Tea and Coffee Co 115
Macy's 87
Manny's 59
Marks and Spencer 81
Matsuda 65
Maud Frizon 55
Mercedes-Benz 65
MOMA Design Store 49, 63, 67
Movado 55
Murray-Hill Antique Center Inc. 111
Mysterious Bookshop 39
New York Bound Bookshop 61
New York Deli 39
OMO Norma Kamali 51
Park Avenue Liquor Shop 91
Paul Stuart 81
Place des Antiquaires 55
Quong Zuen Shing 125
Ralph Lauren 31
Raoul's Boucherie and Charcuterie 123
Rita Ford's Music Boxes 41
Rizzoli Bookstore 51, 123
Rosa Esman 123
Rossi 125
Sally Hawkins Gallery 123
Sandlers Sweet Shop 49
Saki Fifth Avenue 73
Sam Ash 59
Sarge's 101
Schirmer Music Store 33
Scribner's 73
Sea Gull 61
Second Avenue Deli 121
Sky Books 63
SoHotel 123
Spear and Co 97
Stage Deli 47

Steuben Glass 53
Surma 121
Susan Bennis/Warren Edwards 65
T. Anthony 55
TKTS Booth 59
T. O. Dey 91
Tak Sung Tung 125
Tinsel Trading Co 77
Tiny Doll House 67
Teuscher Chocolatier 61
Tiffany's 53
Train Shop, The 71
Urban Center Books 63
Vesuvio's 123
William Hunrach 55
William N. Ginsburg 77
Zabar's 35
Società
San Gennaro 125
South Street Seaport 129
Pier '17' 129
stations
Grand Central 73, 75, 83, 93
Penn 85
Pennsylvania 85

T

theaters
Alvin 45
American Theater of Actors 37
Apple Core 113
Barrymore 43
Booth 57
Boyce 113
Broadway 45
Cherry Lane, Greenwich 115
Circle in the Square 45
Eugene O'Neill 43
Gershwin 45
Lyceum 59
Mitzi E. Newhouse 33
Neil Simon 45
New York State 33
Provincetown Playhouse 117
Shubert 57
Sullivan Street Playhouse 117
Vivian Beaumont 33
Winter Garden 45
Ziegfeld 49
Titanic Memorial Lighthouse 129
Town Hall (New York) 69
United Nations Headquarters 105
Vocational Rehabilitation Agency 109

W

World Trade Center 127

Y

YMCA 35

Z

Zoo, Central Park 49
Zoo, Children's 41

PEOPLE OF INTEREST

A

Allen, Woody 47, 67
Armani 51
Astaire, Fred 45
Astor family 63
Astor, Mrs William 41, 97
Astor, William Waldorf 97

B

Bankhead, Tallulah 65
Barrymore, Ethel 43, 59
Beatles, The 51
Beaumont, Vivian 37
Benchley, Robert 71
Bennett, James Gordon 87
Bernstein, Leonard 39
Bobst, Elmer Holmes 119
Bogardus 129
Breuer, Marcel 31
Brumidi, Constantine 109
Burgee, John 129

C

Calder, Alexander 59
Calder, I. Stirling 59
Carnegie, Andrew 29
Carrre and Hastings 29, 53, 79
Caruso, Enrico 69
Castellano, Paul 95
Chaplin, Charlie 61
Clarke, Thomas 113
Cohen, George 59
Cooper, Peter 29, 121
Corbett, Raymond R. 109
Coutan, Jules 93
Cushman, Don Alonzo 113

D

Duke, James B. 31
Davis and Brody 37
Duckworth, Isaac F. 123
Duffy, Francis 59

F

Fernbach, Henry 65
Fisher, Avery 33
Fitzgerald, F. Scott 101
Fitzgerald, Zelda Scott 100
Flagg, Ernest 123
Forgione, Larry 109
Forrest, Edwin 113, 121
Fox and Fowle 129
French, Daniel Chester 131
French, Fred F. 81, 103
Frick, Henry Clay 29, 31

G

Gallo, Joey 125
Gaynor, James P. 123
Gershwin, George 79, 121
Gilbert, C. P. H. 99
Gilbert, Cass 131

Glaser, Milton 39, 73, 111
Goodhue, Bertram 75
Goodman, Benny 29
Goodwillie, Frank 109
Graham, Ernest 127
Gray, Eileen 49
Gresley, Horace 87
Guggenheim 29

H

Hale, Nathan 81
Hardenbergh, Henry J. 51, 97
Harrison, Abramovitz and Harris 45
Haughwout, Eder V. 123
Hearst, William Randolph 109
Helmsley, Harry 63, 83
Helmsley, Leona 63, 83
Herts and Tallant 59
Hitler, Adolf 61
Hoffman, Malvina 111
Holland, George 107
Hood, Raymond 89
Hopper, Edward 49
Howells and Hood 103
Hunt, Richard Morris 31, 123, 127

J

James, Henry 119
Javits, Jacob 85
Jefferson, Joseph 107
Johnson and Foster 119
Johnson, Philip 49, 65, 67, 129
Jolson, Al 45
Jones, Lowell 83

K

Kahn, Otto 29
Koenig, Fritz 127
Kohn, Robert 35
Kooning, de 49
Krapp, Herbert J. 43

L

Lacroix 51
Lanier, James F. D. 111
Lauren, Ralph 31, 51
Le Corbusier, Charles 49, 105
Lennon, John 35
Lichtenstein, Roy 45
Luciano, Lucky 75

M

McBean, Thomas 127
McKim, Mead and White 31, 41, 63, 69, 71, 75, 79, 85, 87, 93, 97, 99, 107, 109, 117
Macready, William 121
Magonigle and Piccirilli 39
Mandel, Henry 37
Marantz, Irving 111
Marsh, Reginald 131
Martinez, Zarela 67
Matisse, Henri 49
Merman, Ethel 45
Millay, Edna St Vincent 115

Miller, Arthur 43
Monroe, Marilyn 59, 65
Morgan, J. P. 41, 99
Morris, Philip 81
Murray, Mrs 99
Murray, Robert 99

N

Nesbitt, Evelyn 107
Newhouse, Mitzi E. 33

O

O'Neill, Eugene 43, 97, 117

P

Palmer, Charles 55
Parker, Dorothy 71
Pelli, Caesar 49
Picasso, Pablo 49, 65
Pickford, mary 59
Plant, Mrs Morton F. 63
Ponsella, Rosa 59
Porter, Cole 75
Post, George B. 131
Price, Bruce 127
Putnam, Andre 99

R

Rapp and Rapp 57
Reed and Stem 93
Renwick, James 121
Renwick, James Jr 63, 109
Rhind, J. Massey 127
Rich, Charles A. 89
Robb, J. Hampton 111
Roche, Dinkeloo and Associates 31, 45, 49, 95
Rockefeller, John D. 105, 131
Rockefeller, John D. Jr 61, 63, 67
Rockefeller, Nelson 63
Rohe, Mies van der 65
Roth, Emery 71
Rothko, Mark 49, 109
Rubell, Steve 79, 99
Russo, Gaetano 39

S

Saarinen, Eero 49
Schermerhorn, Peter 129
Schrager, Ian 43
Seton, Elizabeth Ann 131
Shepard, Margaret Vanderbilt 41
Silver, H. Percy 99
Simon, Neil 43, 45
Sinatra, Frank 61, 75
Skidmore, Owings and Merrill 55, 65, 71, 73, 75, 79, 127
Sniffen, John 111
Starck, Philippe 39, 79
Starett, Goldwin 71
Stubbins, Hugh 67
Stuyvesant, Peter 121
Swasey, W. A. 45

T

Tchaikovsky, Peter Ilich 39
Tioffany 39
Trumbull, Edward 93
Tully, Alice 33

U

Upjohn, Richard 127

V

Van Alen 41
Vanderbilt family 63, 75
Vaux, Calvert 31
Villard, Henry 63

W

Warhol, Andy 109
Warren and Wetmore 29, 51, 71, 83, 93, 109
Washington, George 131
Weaver, Warren 119
Wells, James N. 113
White, Stanford 75, 107, 111, 119
Whitney, Payne 31
Windsor, Duchess of 75
Winston, Harry 51
Wright, Frank Lloyd 29, 51, 65

STREET INDEX

A

Amsterdam Avenue 32, 35
Ann Street 126, 128
Astor Place 121
Avenue of the Americas/Sixth Avenue 44, 48-9, 50, 58, 59, 60, 68, 69, 70, 71, 72, 76, 78, 86, 88, 96, 116
Avenue South, The 114

B

Barclay Street 126
Barrow Street 114
Battery Place 130
Baxter Street 124
Bayard Street 124
Baynard[?] Street 125
Beaver Street 130
Bedford Street 114, 115
Beekman Street 128
Bleecker Street 114, 115, 116, 118
Bowery, The 120, 124, 125
Bridge Street 130
Broad Street 130
Broadway 32, 35, 38, 39, 42, 44, 45, 46, 47, 56, 58, 68, 69, 76, 77, 86, 96, 106, 118, 121, 122, 124, 126, 128, 130
  West 122, 123
Broome Street 122, 124
Burling Slip 128

C

Canal Street 124, 125
Carmine Street 114
Center Drive 50
Centre Market Place 124
Central Park Place 37
Central Park South 38, 50, 51, 52
Central Park West 32, 34-5, 38
Centre Street 124
Christopher Street 114, 115
Church Street 126
Clarkson Street 114
Cleveland Place 122
Cliff Street 128
Coentjes Alley 130
Coentjes Slip 130
Columbus Avenue 32, 34, 35
Columbus Circle 32, 34, 37, 38-9
Commerce Street 114, 115
Cooper Square 120
Cornelia Street 114, 116
Cortlandt Street 126
Crosby Street 122, 124
Cushman Row 113

D

Dey Street 126
Downing Street 114
Duffey Square 59

E

8th Street
  East 118, 119, 120
  West 118, 119
11th Street East 120
18th Street West 112
80th Street 35
82nd Street 30
84th Street East 28
85th Street East 28
86th Street East 28
87th Street East 28
88th Street East 28
89th Street East 28
East Drive 40
Eighth Avenue 36, 42, 44, 45, 46, 47, 56, 84, 85, 112
Elizabeth Street 124, 125
Exchange Place 130

F

4th Street
  East 120
  West 116, 117, 118
5th Street East 120
14th Street West 112
15th Street West 112
40th Street
  East 78, 90, 92, 98, 100, 102
  West 68, 76, 77, 78, 88, 89, 90, 98
41st Street
  East 80, 90, 92, 94, 98, 110, 102, 104
  West 68, 76, 88
42nd Street
  East 78, 80-1, 82, 90, 92, 93, 94, 95, 100, 102-3, 104
  West 56, 57, 68, 69, 70, 76, 78, 79, 88, 90
43rd Street
  East 80, 81, 82, 90, 92, 94, 102, 104
  West 56, 68, 70, 78, 79, 80
44th Street
  East 80, 81, 82, 90, 92, 94, 102, 104
  West 56, 57, 58, 59, 68, 70, 71, 78, 79, 80
45th Street
  East 72, 80, 82, 83, 92, 94, 95, 104
  West 56, 58, 59, 68, 70, 71, 78, 80
46th Street
  East 72, 80, 82, 92, 94, 95, 104
  West 42, 56, 57, 58, 60, 68, 70, 78, 80
47th Street
  East 72, 74, 80, 82, 94, 104
  West 42, 43, 56, 57, 58, 60, 70, 71
48th Street
  East 60, 62, 72, 73, 74, 82, 94, 105
  West 42, 44, 56, 58, 59, 60, 70, 72
49th Street
  East 62, 66, 72, 73, 74, 82, 105
  West 42, 43, 44, 58, 60, 61, 70, 72
50th Street
  East 62, 66, 72, 74-5
  West 42, 43, 44, 58, 60, 62, 72
51st Street
  East 62, 64, 66, 72, 74
  West 42, 43, 44, 45, 46, 48, 60, 62, 72
52nd Street
  East 62, 63, 64, 66, 67, 72, 74

West 36, 42, 44, 45, 46, 48, 60, 62
53rd Street
  East 53, 62, 64, 66, 74
  West 35, 36, 42, 44, 46, 48, 49, 60,
    62
54th Street
  East 52, 53, 62, 64, 65, 66, 74
  West 36, 37, 38, 44, 46, 48, 62
55th Street
  East 52, 53, 62, 64, 66, 67, 74
  West 36, 38, 44, 46, 48, 49, 50, 52, 62, 63
56th Street
  East 52, 54, 64, 66
  West 36, 38, 46, 47, 48, 50, 51, 52
57th Street 53
  East 52, 53, 54, 55, 64, 65
  West 36, 37, 38, 39, 46, 48, 50-1, 52
58th Street
  East 52, 53, 54, 64
  West 32, 36, 38, 39, 46, 50, 51, 52
59th Street
East 52, 54, 55
  West 32, 36, 40
Father Demo Square 116
Fifth Avenue 28, 29, 30, 40, 48, 50-1, 52, 53, 60,
    62, 63, 70-1, 72-3, 78, 80-1, 88-9, 90, 96, 98,
    104, 106, 118, 119
First Avenue 102, 104, 120
Fletcher Street 128
Fourth Avenue 120
Franklin Delano Roosevelt Drive 104
Front Street 128
Fulton Street 126, 128, 129

G

Gold Street 128
Grand Army Plaza 52
Grand Street 122, 124, 125
Great Enmore Street 124
Greeley Square 87
Greene Street 118, 122, 123
Greenwich Street 126, 127
Grove Court 115
Grove Street 114

H

Hanover Square 131
Harry Howard Square 124
Herald Square 86-7, 96
Hester Street 124, 125
Houston Street West 114, 116, 122, 123
Howard Street 124
Hudson Street 114

J

James N. Wells Row 113
Jeanette Park 130
John Street 128, 129
Jones Street 114

K

Kenmore Park 122

L

La Guardia Place 116, 118
Lafayette Street 122, 124
Leroy Street 114
Lexington Avenue 28, 54, 64, 66, 74, 75, 82, 92,
    93, 94, 95, 98, 100, 108, 109, 110
Liberty Street 126, 127, 128
Lincoln Square 32, 34, 35
Longacre Square 69

M

MacDougal Alley 118, 119
MacDougal Street 116, 117
Madison Avenue 28, 30, 31, 40, 41, 51, 52, 54, 55,
    62, 64, 72, 73, 74, 80, 82, 90, 91, 99, 106,
    108, 109
Maiden Lane 126, 128, 129
Mercer Street 122, 118
Miller Street 118
Ninetta Lane 116
Minetta Street 116
Morris Street 130
Morton Street 114, 115
Mott Street 125
Mulberry Street 124, 125
Murray Street 129

N

9th Street East 118, 120
19th Street West 112
90th Street East 28
91st Street East 28
92nd Street East 28
93rd Street East 28
Nassau Street 126, 128
New Street 130
Ninth Avenue 36, 37, 42, 43, 56, 112
North Street 124

P

Park Avenue 28, 30, 40, 52, 54, 55, 62, 64, 65, 72,
    73, 74-5, 80, 82, 83, 90, 93, 98, 100, 101,
    109, 110, 111
  South 108-9
Pearl Street 128, 130
Pell Street 125
Peter Minuit Plaza 130
Pine Street 126, 128, 130
Platt Street 128
Prince Street 122, 123

R

Rector Street 130
Rockefeller Plaza 48, 60, 61

S

6th Street East 120
7th Street East 120
16th Street West 112
17th Street West 112
60th Street
  East 40, 54
  West 32, 36

61st Street
    East 40, 54, 55
    West 32, 33, 34
62nd Street
    East 40, 54
    West 32, 34
63rd Street
    East 40, 54
    West 32, 33, 34
64th Street
    East 40
    West 32, 34, 35, 40
65th Street
    East 40
    West 34, 35
66th Street
    East 40
    West 34
67th Street
    East 40
    West 34
72nd Street East 30
73rd Street East 30
74th Street East 30
75th Street East 30
76th Street East 30
77th Street East 30
78th Street East 30
79th Street 35
    East 30
St Luke's Place 114
St Mark's Place 120, 121
Schermerhorn Row 129
Second Avenue 66, 94, 102, 104, 105, 111, 120
Seventh Avenue 38, 39, 44, 45, 46, 47, 58, 59, 68,
    76, 84, 85, 86
Seventh Avenue South 114
Sixth Avenue 114, 117
Sixth Avenue/Avenue of the Americas 44, 48-9, 50,
    58, 59, 60, 68, 69, 70, 71, 72, 76, 78, 86, 88,
    96, 116
Sniffen Court 111
South Ferry 130
South Street 129, 130
Spring Street 122
Spruce Street 128
State Street 130
Stone Street 130
Stuyvesant Street 120, 121
Sullivan Street 116, 117

T

3rd Street West 116, 117, 118
10th Street East 118, 120, 121
12th Street East 120
20th Street West 112
21st Street West 112, 113
22nd Street West 112, 113
25th Street
    East 107
    West 106
26th Street 106
27th Street
    East 108

West 106
28th Street
    East 106, 108, 109
    West 85, 106, 107
29th Street
    East 106, 108
    West 84, 106
30th Street
    East 106, 108, 109, 110
    West 84, 85, 106
31st Street
    East 108, 109, 110
    West 84, 85, 86, 96, 106
32nd Street
    East 97, 108, 109, 110
    West 84, 86, 87, 96, 106
33rd Street
    East 96, 98, 108, 110
    West 84, 86, 96
34th Street
    East 96, 98, 108, 110, 111
    West 84, 86, 96, 97
35th Street
    East 98, 99, 100, 110, 111
    West 84, 86, 88, 96, 97
36th Street
    East 90, 98, 100, 110
    West 76, 84, 86, 88, 96, 97
37th Street
    East 90, 98, 100, 102, 110
    West 76, 77, 86, 88, 89, 96, 98
38th Street
    East 90, 98, 100, 102
    West 76, 77, 88, 96, 98
39th Street
    East 90, 91, 92, 98, 100, 101, 102
    WEst 76, 78, 88, 89, 98
Third Avenue 64, 66, 67, 74, 75, 82,
    92, 94, 100, 102, 103, 105, 110, 120
Thompson Street 116, 122
Times Square 43, 56, 57, 58-9, 68-9, 107
Transverse Road No 1 34, 40
Trinity Place 126, 127
Tudor City Place 95

U

United Nations Plaza 104
University Place 118

V

Vanderbilt Avenue 80, 82, 92
Varick Street 114
Vesey Street 126

W

Walker Street 124
Wall Street 126, 127, 128, 130
Washington Mews 119
Washington Place 116, 117, 118
Washington Square 116, 117, 118-19
Washington Square East 118
Washington Square North 118, 119
Washington Square South 116, 118
Washington Square Village 118, 119

INDEX OF STREET NAMES

Washington Square West 116
Washington Street 126, 129
Water Street 128, 130
Waverly Place 116, 118
West Drive 34, 38
West End Avenue 35
West Washington Place 116
Whitehall Street 130
William Street 128
William Street South 130
Wooster Street 122